SAVE
TOBY!

D1489021

SAVE TOBY!

Buy This Book or the Bunny Dies

James and Brian

CITADEL PRESS
Kensington Publishing Corp.
www.kensingtonbooks.com

Dedicated to Toby,
he's a fighter that's for sure.

PUBLISHER'S NOTE
May be hazardous to crazy liberal hippie animal activists.

CITADEL PRESS BOOKS are published by

Kensington Publishing Corp.
850 Third Avenue
New York, NY 10022

All Kensington titles, imprints, and distributed lines are available at
special quantity discounts for bulk purchases for sales promotions, premi-
ums, fund-raising, educational, or institutional use. Special book excerpts
or customized printings can also be created to fit specific needs. For
details, write or phone the office of the Kensington special sales manager:
Kensington Publishing Corp., 850 Third Avenue, New York, NY 10022,
attn: Special Sales Department; phone 1-800-221-2647.

CITADEL PRESS and the Citadel logo are Reg. U.S. Pat. & TM Off.

First printing: September 2005

10 9 8 7 6 5 4 3 2 1

Printed in the United States of America

CIP data is available.

ISBN 0-8065-2761-7

Contents

Congratulations...

CONGRATULATIONS ON YOUR PURCHASE OF *SAVE TOBY!* You have just contributed in an important way to the survival of the greatest bunny of all time and maybe even the greatest in all the animal kingdom, or phyla. Every book counts toward the goal of 100,000 sold (net!) that will save Toby's life. You are also contributing in an important way to the book publishing industry, which might be in even more trouble than Toby! But before Toby's life depended on selling 100,000 copies of a book, his life was ransomed on the Internet for $50,000. That didn't work out so well, but *not* because people didn't want to save him. You see, certain grouchy people petitioned PayPal, saying mean things like, "You can't let this crime against God and humanity continue." Then the nice, caring people who wanted to save Toby couldn't donate because the Save Toby! account was frozen. The grouches almost prevented Toby from getting saved. But then we got another idea—there's no way PayPal can freeze a book! It's one last chance to save Toby, and it's so crazy it might work. But if it doesn't, Toby *will* be butchered and eaten; so maybe you should pick up two or three copies?

Before Toby

WE DIDN'T JUST ROLL OUT OF BED ONE MORNING AND COME UP WITH THE IDEA TO RANSOM A BUNNY'S LIFE ON THE INTERNET FOR $50,000. No, cruelty and extortion have been lifelong passions for both of us. As a child, Brian here threatened to kill and eat his sister's Monchhichi if he wasn't given ice cream; as a schoolboy, James would threaten to eat your homework unless you gave him your lunch money. The day we met at fat camp, a dream was born.

When we started working together, all we knew was that we wanted fifty thousand dollars. It took us many failed attempts to find exactly the right hostage for our Save Toby! campaign.

STINKY, THE DUNG BEETLE

We didn't raise any money at all. On the plus side, though, we now have a nice ball of dung.

TOBY, THE SOCIALLY LIBERAL, FISCALLY CONSERVATIVE COLUMNIST FOR *The New York Times*

Again, no money came. We released him into the wild, and he now blogs for www.huffingtonpost.com.

TO-BI-OH! THE ANIME HERO

Who could resist Tobi, with his crazy adventures and his huge, manga

eyes? Unfortunately, he was kidnapped by confused fanboys who thought he was Sailor Moon.

TOBY, THE CHUPACABRA

When we captured the legendary Mexican half-alien, half-dinosaur vampire, we couldn't believe our luck. Finally, something people would want to save! Unfortunately, Toby Chupacabra escaped from his cage, drank our blood, and left us for dead. Again, no money.

TOBY, THE STICK INSECT

This also didn't work. In an irony of Batesian mimicry, nobody wanted to save Toby's life, because they thought he was just a stick.

TOBY, THE ADORABLE BLACK MIDGET KID

We never understood why this worked so well for *Diff'rent Strokes* and *Webster*, but didn't work for us. We wrote and produced seventeen original 22-minute "webisodes," co-starring football legend and surprisingly affordable Hall of Famer Howie Long. In every episode, Toby would learn a valuable lesson about life, then everybody would hug, then Howie Long would threaten to kill Toby and eat him if we didn't get paid $50,000. This one really should have worked.

TOBY, THE BONOBO

It wasn't easy getting our hands on one of these legendarily sex-crazed primates. We thought, *Great, sex sells! This time, everyone will want to Save Toby!* We put a webcam in his cage, but the bonobo had sex with the camera. We tried putting the webcam outside the cage, but Toby escaped, had sex with the camera again, then had sex with our Ikea lamp and our authentic Thomas Kincaid print with customized highlights applied by a former apprentice to the

master himself. The bonobo escaped into the wild, and we never found out what happened to him. Overall, our bonobo adventure was a complete disaster, and we didn't get any money at all, apart from an envelope we found in his cage stuffed with $10,000 cash and a note that said I LOVE YOU, BUT I'M MARRIED TO THE SEA, which we still don't understand.

TOBY, THE HUMAN PAPILLOMA VIRUS

Man, this was a terrible idea. We were thinking, *Hey, not only can we make money on the Internet by threatening to murder a virus, at the same time we can also educate people about an STD that can cause cervical cancer!* Okay, I know that idea seems stupid when you look at it in black and white, but you've got to remember this was 1999. The Internet was different then.

TOBY, THE FRAGGLE

You know how on *Fraggle Rock*, the Fraggles and the Doozers got along for the most part? And you know how they never had an episode where a Fraggle and a Doozer were both put in the same cage, and two hours later you discovered that the Doozers immobilized the Fraggles with a neurotoxin you didn't even know they secreted, and then the Doozers ate out the Fraggles' eyes? I wish they had made an episode like that.

TOBEY MAGUIRE

No luck.

TOBY, THE LIGER

We had to quickly abandon this plan after we were sued by Kellogg's, the producers of *Napoleon Dynamite*, and a tigon.

Postmortem Merchandise

WE'RE IN THIS TO MAKE MONEY—LOTS OF IT. So how can we leverage a fully matured, vertically integrated extortion product into explosive growth? What are the out-of-the-hutch ancillary opportunities we're not realizing? After Toby is eaten, how will we not only operate the Save Toby! profit-making machine, but actually take it to the next level?

Problem? Solution! In the event that *Save Toby!* does not sell 100,000 copies, you will be able to buy merchandise actually made from Toby! Think of them as mementos of your failure to save him.

The Native Americans were famous for not wasting any part of buffalo, and we will not waste any part of Toby. And you have our personal assurance that each item we sell comes from the one, true, original Toby.

ITEM	DESCRIPTION	PRICE
Toby's Lucky Rabbit Foot	Limit: 8 per customer. Feeling lucky, punk? With one of Toby's feet in your pocket, the answer will be "Heck yes I do!" *All in!*	$60 EACH
Toby Jerky	Sure, we plan on eating Toby, but there will be leftovers. Please specify original, black pepper, or teriyaki.	$14 PER STRIP
Yukon Barbie's Trapper Coat	You know how that bitch Brianna thinks she's better than you? Well, wait until she sees the world's only doll coat made out of Toby. She'll scratch out her own eyes with envy.	$100
"Toby or Not to Be"—The FUN New Board Game!	It's just like the shell game, except you play with one of Toby's toes. Unless you're a big fan of puns, you should probably pass this one by.	$16
Toby Prada Bag	It's the perfect nightclub accessory. Nothing says "fashionista" like a bag made out of a real Internet celebrity. Think of it as bunny clubbing!	$900
Toby Toothpicks	These toothpicks made from Toby's bones really come in handy, especially when you're picking Toby Jerky out of your teeth.	$22

Toby's Whiskers	Most people don't know this, but it's actually the whiskers that make a bunny cute. If you buy these, you can glue them to your face and get into any nightclub in town	**$23**
Toby's Spleen	Rabbit spleens are aphrodisiacs in many countries. Well, not many countries. Just Brunei. And it's because the Sultan of Brunei is a superfreak. So, Sultan, call us, okay? That night at the party, you said you'd call us and we'd all hang out, but you never called.	**$50 EACH**
Toby's Corneas	You're getting older! Someday your eyes will get cloudy and you'll need new corneas. So why hope against hope for an organ donor when Toby's got two shiny new corneas for you *today*? While it's true that implanting rabbit corneas would make you a chimera unrecognizable as human by God himself, you'd also have adorable bunny eyes! Totally worth it.	**$100 EACH**
Toby Bouillon Cubes	You'll be saying "Boo-yah" to these bouillon cubes!	**$3**
Toby's Soul	You might be thinking that rabbits don't have souls. But they do. It's in the Old Testament.	**$500**

Toby's Death Cries CD	Shock all your bourgeois friends. *Darkest Hour* is like "Don't Worry, Be Happy" compared to this stuff.	**$19.95 OR $1 PER TRACK AT THE APPLE STORE**
Toby's Rabbit Ears and Tail	Planning to out-slut all of your sorority sisters this Halloween? Duh! But why dress up as an ordinary "bunny" when you can be a famous one? You'll finally get noticed by a Sigma Chi, and your morning-after walk of shame will be a stride of pride	**$75**
Toby's Genitals	Now why would we sell that? What's wrong with you?	**GET HELP.**

If We Get Close . . .

TOBY IS CUTE, BUT IF YOU PEOPLE COME UP EVEN ONE BOOK SHORT OF 100,000 COPIES, WE WILL EAT HIM UP. However, we are not unreasonable people, and we are grateful for every book sold. We don't want you to feel like your contribution was wasted if the final tally falls short, so here is the deal we're offering: The more books we sell, the nicer we will be to Toby before he dies. Here's the breakdown:

5,000 books	We'll buy Toby a little leather bunny suit and go cruising in the S&M district. How do we know that Toby is into S&M? We don't—most bunnies aren't. How is this making Toby's life better? It's really not. So you probably want to make sure we sell more than 5,000 copies.
10,000 books	We'll take him for one last dinner with his family. He can have a touching farewell with his mother and father. He can tell them how much he loves them both.
15,000 books	We'll rent a helicopter for a day and go on an aerial adventure with our furry friend. The greatest fantasy for most bunnies is that they could fly (except for the few that are into S&M).
20,000 books	We'll honor Toby with a Friars Club roast, hosted by Jim Breuer (he's available.) After the roast, we'll roast.
25,000 books	We will re-create the final scene of the musical *Annie*, where Annie is reunited with Daddy Warbucks, in which Toby will play Annie.
30,000 books	We will throw Toby a rave. We will drop a glow-stick into his cage, put on some Chemical Brothers, and put a couple of tabs of Ecstasy in his drinking bottle.
40,000 books	Most people don't know this, but Make-A-Wish completely turned their backs on Toby, even though he has a terminal illness called "not enough books sold." However, with the royalties from 40,000 books in hand, we can finally make Toby's wish come true. Unfortunately, Toby's wish is to kill a dog.

60,000 books	We'll take Toby to Boys Town, Nuevo Laredo, to see a donkey show. Because you know bunnies, they loves them a donkey show.
70,000 books	We'll fly in a harem of seventy female bunnies from around the globe; we'll cover the walls with black crushed velvet and play Ravel's *Bolero*. It will be a week Toby will never forget for the remainder of his brief life, assuming he's male. I've been guessing he is, but I really don't know that much about rabbits.
99,999 books	Wow. This is a moral dilemma. I know we said that if we came even one book short, that we would eat Toby. But it's one thing to say it, and another thing to see it written down like this. Suddenly, I feel cold. Are we not all brothers in the eyes of a loving God? Toby, you are my brother. If it takes just one more book to spare your life, then I will buy that book myself. I'm assuming that I can find a copy at the local bookstore—I am not going to buy online—but except for that, I will not let an innocent bunny die for the want of one measly book.
99,998 books	Two books, though . . . different story.

Hate Mail

FOR SOME REASON, AS MANY PEOPLE AS THERE ARE WHO LOVE TOBY and want to save him, there seem to be even more people who are mad at us for trying to save him. It doesn't make much sense to us, either.

Here are some samples of the kind of hate mail we get every day.

HEY BUNGHOLE,

You wanna eat something? How about you eat me! You think you're pretty funny, huh? Guess what? I'm gonna rescue a rug and start a website demanding I get paid or I will MUNCH CARPET! How do you like that? I'd put you right out of business. Everyone will come to my website and they'll forget about yours. Pervert.

Bite me,
TUCKER

My Dear Hellbound Friend:

First off, I am a born-again Christian and I am appalled by what you are doing. May God have mercy on your soul. I wish to extend an invitation to you to join me in fellowship so that you may see your way beyond these demons that have obviously taken command of your life. Fortunately, the Lord has provided technology that will allow you to join us from any location on earth via the World Wide Web. It is obvious to me that you are able to use the Internet, so you must follow my instructions carefully.

Here is what is needed: The Lord desires for you to transfer all proceeds from *Save Toby!* into our church's PayPal account. Then—and only then—will He forgive your sins and wash you clean forever, allowing you to rise from the pits of eternal fire.

Eternally yours,
Louie "Ace" Roggio

Dear Mr. Killer,

My name is Amie Anderson and I am in Miss Hall's first period class. We are having an assignment to make the world a better place. What you are doing is mean and you should stop it. If you do then the world would not be as bad as it was before. If you do not then it will be worse and I will probably get a bad grade on this assignment. Plus I love bunnies and if you don't want Toby I will take him. He is so cute. My dad says you are going to be punished for what you are doing, but he didn't tell me how. You should let Toby go and not eat him because he probably doesn't taste very good anyway. My mom could make you some chicken that's really good if you want. Tell me when you are coming over so I can tell my mom.

Bye,
Amie Anderson

Dear Save Toby,

First of all, I should tell you that I am from the future. You're just going to have to trust me on this when I tell you that you need to release Toby. The future of the world depends on it. Toby has been chosen by destiny to lead mankind from the brink of nuclear war. If he is slain, the world will collapse and the evil Lord Cadbury will achieve his dream of world domination. This CANNOT happen. Lord Cadbury has targeted the United States as his number-one enemy. **WE WILL ALL DIE IF YOU DO NOT RELEASE TOBY!** Also, if you could please send me a free T-shirt I'd appreciate it. I'm a **XXXL**.

Thanks a bunch,

E-Ron

Dear Anguished People,

You should know that these acts of barbarianism will not give you what you so desperately wish to achieve—the love of your mother. Is it that you see <u>yourself</u> in Toby? Isn't it <u>you</u> that you want to kill and eat? Just think about it, that's all.

Sincerely,

PROFESSOR QUACKENBUSH

To: Save Toby! ATTN: Toby
From: Ebunny@choccity.com
Subject: What a tired act...

Dear Toby,

Easter Bunny here with a message: Give it up already! Seriously. There have been many martyrs before you, and only one has been successfully resurrected. We all know that it was my boss, Jesus Christ, who died on the cross for our sins. I mean J.C. could turn water into wine! Do you really think you can turn carrots into carats?

For years, I have been associated with delicious candy eggs. Rabbits don't lay eggs, let alone tasty chocolate ones. How do you think I pulled that off? By busting my cottontail! If your little stunt has a negative impact on my career, I'm dragging you down to the bottom.

Don't think it's just me who has a problem with you; fur is flying throughout the entire celebrity rabbit community. We've worked too long and too hard for respect just to let some interloper with a get-rich-quick scheme ruin our careers.

Can you imagine "Silly jellyfish, Trix are for kids!" Or Elmer Fudd hunting a "Wascally Wing-Tailed Wemur?" Do you want to see the Energizer Bunny banging that drum and marching all the way to the unemployment line? Stop being selfish and start thinking about the consequences of your actions.

Sincerely,
The Easter Bunny

From: JCs3rv3nt
Subject: please repent

Dear Toby's owner,

Please do not consider this "hate mail" because I do not hate you; I pity you. Be sure that Toby is a creature of God, and any harm you do unto him will be revisited upon your soul. That is unless you give yourself to your Lord.

I would hate for someone to rig a detonator to your ignition, causing a bar of C4 to roast you inside your 1998 Montero Sport, license plate OGICU812B4 . . . because it would be but a taste of the suffering you will endure in your afterlife.

Please consider getting saved, and please visit our church, located on Spring St. We're having a bake sale on Saturday afternoon (bring some cookies to be entered in the raffle), Super Sunday service is at 8 am and 12 pm with rocking Pastor James, and Tuesday is singles night.

Your friend in Jesus,
Eileen

May 24, 2005
The Founders
Save Toby, Inc.
www.savetoby.com

To whom it may concern:

On behalf of PATE, the second-largest animal rights organization in the world, and its more than 800,000 members, this letter is the proverbial shot across Save Toby's bow.

Founded in 1980, PATE is dedicated to establishing and protecting the rights of all animals. We operate under the simple principle that animals are not ours to eat, wear, experiment on, or use for entertainment. Your website, www.savetoby.com, is terrorist in nature, and the instant you described Toby, your companion animal, as a "pet," war was declared. I consider your institution's existence a direct infringement upon the precious ideals my organization was created to foster.

As I'm sure you're aware, PATE's influence grows by the day with every pliable teenage mind that we manage to mold into our very own vegan sentinel. Our foot soldiers span the globe and include the rich, powerful, and famous. We've collaborated with actor Alec Baldwin on a video entitled <u>Meet Your Meat</u>, which parlayed his reputation for paparazzi punching into a powerful look at the life cycle of an animal that's being raised for food. We've also joined forces with longtime PATE spokesperson Pamela Anderson, who, at the likely expense of her own well-being, heroically took the place of chimpanzees in Southern California's Silicone Implant Testing Facility.

I've always drawn inspiration from the renowned humanitarian Dr. Albert Schweitzer, who accomplished so much for both humans and animals in his lifetime and was known to take time to stoop and move a worm from hot pavement to cool earth. This man, God rest his soul, is the embodiment of everything I believe. Before you even contemplate proceeding with your declared dastardly deed, I urge you first to read <u>You Can Save the Animals: 251 Simple Ways to Stop Thoughtless Cruelty</u>. I penned this book as a young girl while raiding black market dog pounds in the alleys of New Delhi.

Recent victories for PATE over corporate offenders include lawsuits forcing KFC to stop lying about conditions for their chickens and General Electric to replace animal-based tests with methods that don't use them. (Although KFC has filed a countersuit stating that they have never used real chicken in the first place, so this specific example may become moot.) And many sponsors, including MasterCard, have agreed to no longer back the Ringling Bros. and Barnum & Bailey Circus, thus improving the likelihood that the Yak Woman will eventually gain her right to freedom.

Will Save Toby, Inc. be the next (synthetic) feather in PATE's cap? Only you can decide.

Sincerely yours,

Kirk Ingnew
Co-founder and President
PATE

Here is an excellent article written by Mr. Antoine Tyler that appeared in the July 2005 issue of Gentlemen's Semiannual *magazine.*

$50,000 Is Not Enough If You're Living Right!

by Antoine Tyler, Lifestyle Consultant to the Stars

LET ME LAY IT DOWN FOR YOU on how easy it would be to blow fifty grand on a rabbit. Now, according to a study by the British animal charity Blue Cross, a typical rabbit can cost

about $5,000 to feed and maintain over the course of its natural lifespan, which is between 9 and 12 years. So we might think that $50,000 is a bit extreme, and that maybe these "Save Toby!" guys are just trying to line their own pockets.

But get this: That study was for the cost of keeping a typical rabbit, right? I've met Toby, and I'm here to say that this rabbit is anything but typical. He's got class, savoir-faire, and a taste for the finer things. It's plain to see how easy it would be to spend fifty large on giving Toby the kind of lifestyle he deserves.

I'll break it down for you. Toby's needs are going to fall into four categories: habitat, food, grooming, and healthcare. First up is habitat. Most pet care experts will recommend that a rabbit be kept in a cage that allows 5 square feet of room per rabbit. Toby don't play like that. He's gonna need much more space. In fact, I've worked up a layout that uses an entire room. It's part hutch, part above-ground warren. The hutch itself is made of cedar, but the cedar is layered over 5-inch thick steel plate. This is the panic room of rabbit hutches. You could drop a bunker buster on this mother and it wouldn't make a dent. It has an independent heating and cooling system, built in air filters, a back-up oxygen supply, and motion-sensitive activators. Toby is a celebrity, and security is foremost.

Now, the hutch itself is pretty impressive, but the warren is what's really cool. I know the guy who made Richard Gere's gerbil habitat, and he used the same design, only tripled the size. Plus, the guy's name actually is Warren, so he knows what he's doing. Toby's gonna flip. Total cost: $26,490, not including maintenance and wood chips.

Next is food. Rabbit dieticians agree that plenty of fresh dark green vegetables are best for a rabbit's diet. In fact, carrots are discouraged, because they have too much water and give a rabbit the runs. Anyway, alfalfa is the vegetable of choice for keeping a rabbit healthy, happy and regular. A 1- to 2-pound rabbit will eat 12 ounces of alfalfa in a day. If we give Toby the benefit of the doubt and assume he's going to last 12 years (he's going to have plenty to live for), that's 3,285 pounds of alfalfa. Freshness is key. A weekly shipment of alfalfa from an organic farm in Napa is going to run $27, so over the course of 12 years, that's $16,848, for a running total of $43,338.

Rabbits don't groom themselves like cats. Cats are ghetto. Toby's going to need a monthly session with a groomer, 'cause it's lights, camera, and action. His fur and nails will need trimming, his teeth will need whitening, his tail will need fluffening, and his ears will have to be styled at all times, like he just hopped out of *Look* magazine. Estimated cost: $5,750.

We're already near the $50,000 mark, and that's without healthcare. Toby could have an accident, or need an operation, or just want to have some work done to feel better about himself. The main question is going to be whether or not to have him neutered. Even though it may mean robbing him of one of life's greatest pleasures, I've got to recommend neutering Toby. It's either that or settling a lifetime of paternity suits—legitimate or not, the legal costs of fighting them are astronomical. Trust me on this one.

WHY RABBITS DESERVE TO DIE

THERE IS A JAPANESE LEGEND, WHICH STATES THAT SOME RABBITS LIVE ON THE MOON AND MAKE A STICKY RICE-BASED TREAT CALLED MOCHI. This snack is a favorite around New Year's, and every year, a number of people die from choking on it (mostly children and the elderly). So you can see, rabbits are prejudiced murderers.

According to one version of the Arthurian legend, King Arthur and his knights ran afoul of an especially vicious rabbit in their quest for the Holy Grail. This encounter left five knights (that is, three knights) dead, and the rest thoroughly demoralized. The rabbit was eventually dispatched by the Holy Hand Grenade of Antioch, but he was a nasty little beast all the same.

Although the Great Chicago Fire is widely believed to have been started when Mrs. O'Leary's cow knocked over a lantern, many tragedy buffs now speculate that the fire was actually started by her pet rabbit. A well-known animal lover, Mrs. O'Leary kept an extensive menagerie in her shed, including a cow, a rabbit, a duck, an ibex, a komodo dragon, a sloth, a carp, and a fruit bat. On the evening of October 8, 1871, Mrs. O'Leary lit a lantern in the barn where her son James was enjoying a game of Old Maid with his friend Pegleg Sullivan. Pausing briefly to get more cider, Sullivan observed the rabbit as it hopped out of its cage, snuck quietly over to the cow, then jumped noisily on the upturned washtub next to the cow, thus spooking it and causing it to kick over the lantern. As such, we can see that this rabbit was not only an arsonist, but also framed a perfectly innocent cow.

Until the twentieth century, rabbits were included in the order Rodentia, as members of the class Mammalia; that is, until someone decided that rabbits should belong to a different order on the grounds that unlike rodents, they have four incisors in their upper jaw, the male's scrotum is in front of the penis (which does not have a bone as rodents' penises do), and they will re-digest first-time feces to obtain the most from their vegetation-based diet. Rabbits were redefined as members of the order Lagomorpha. As a result of this reclassification, thousands of biology and zoology students failed their midterms, and the publishers of *The Discerning Boulevardier's Compleat Guide to Rodents* had to recall every copy, laying off more than one hundred workers to make up for the lost revenue. Some may argue that this was human error, but these events would not have occurred if rabbits hadn't gone evolving their scrotums all over the place.

A six-foot three-inch invisible rabbit named Harvey gained a certain degree of notoriety in the latter half of the twentieth century.

save toby! 31

Although usually portrayed as little more than a lighthearted imp who enjoys poking fun at the oppressiveness of a strictly conformist society, this rabbit has nonetheless made a practice of appearing to a number of drunks and derelicts throughout the years and is responsible for over a hundred cases of people being wrongfully committed and/or lobotomized.

Fidel Castro was born in the Chinese year of the rabbit and was known to carry a rabbit's foot for luck. He had it with him during his last at-bat for the Havana University baseball team in the big championship game against San Juan. He hit a pop fly to second which lost the game, 7–6. This embittered young Castro, and he later got cozy with the Russians. That led to the failed Bay of Pigs invasion, which severely embarrassed the Kennedy administration. Nice going, rabbit.

Roger Rabbit burst onto the national scene in 1989 as the star of a popular feature film that mixed live action with animation. This film was remarkable because it would be the only time that Warner Bros. and Disney would allow their signature characters to appear together in the same production. This was in the days before both companies began their decade-long descent into soulless greed. In the film, Roger's wife, Jessica, asserts that she likes him because he makes her laugh. This resulted in a large number of impressionable young men choosing to refocus their attention away from physical fitness and good personal hygiene to becoming comedy writers, on the promise that it would attract gorgeous redheads with long legs and huge boobs. So, *thanks* for that.

Extortion Throughout History

THE AUTHORS OF *SAVE TOBY!* HAVE BEEN ACCUSED BY SOME OF THEIR DETRACTORS OF COMMITTING AN ACT OF EXTORTION. Dr. Thomas Gilbert, Ph.D., professor of criminology at St. Barnard's University, puts extortion in a historical context and provides us with some notable examples.

50 B.C.—Sallust attempts to extort money from Senator Berelius

The earliest known record of extortion comes from Ancient Rome, and a member of the Senate named Sallust. Sallust was a historian, and a loyal devotee of Caesar. He was also extremely corrupt, and his historical accounts display a clear bias, particularly with his tendency to refer to other senators as "that asshole," as in "that asshole Marcus Pubilus."

In 50 B.C. Sallust became embroiled in scandal. According to records and private journals, he attempted to extort money from fellow senator Quintus Burelius, threatening that unless Burelius paid him 500 aurei, he would reveal that Burelius engaged in the "unspeakable vice of the Greeks" (a euphemism for goat porking). Burelius refused and openly denounced Sallust, saying that he would rather be known as a goat porker than a *popularis*.

Naturally, the general public found this to be terribly amusing, and Burelius's approval ratings skyrocketed. Sallust's reputation never recovered, and he would have been dismissed from the Senate if not for the direct intervention of Caesar.

1932—The Lindbergh baby

In early February of 1932, world-renowned aviator Charles Lindbergh received threats that harm would befall his son, Charles Jr., unless $20,000 was left in a hollow tree in a park outside Trenton, New Jersey, at a specified time.

Lindbergh notified the authorities, and a fairly routine sting operation was set up. A dummy bag was placed in the tree, and when the extortionists arrived to collect it, they were arrested and imprisoned. The two men, Leon Wadowski and Gerald Keeler, were unemployed news reporters who had planned to use what they considered to be a sensational news story to revive their flagging careers.

They were each sentenced to fifteen years in prison, and were in a cell awaiting trial on March 1 when Charles Lindbergh Jr. was kidnapped from his home. Some authorities attempted to pin the kidnapping on Wadowski and Keeler anyway, but that would have meant suggesting that the two men had broken out of their cell, traveled 17 miles, committed the crime, hid the baby, then returned to their cell and removed any trace of having left, doing so in the 32-minute time-span between when their dinner was brought to them and lights out. This proved not only to be impossible but, more important, would have reflected poorly on the New Jersey law enforcement community, and so the idea fell by the wayside.

"Looking back, we were pretty incompetent," Keeler admitted in a later interview. "Lindy didn't know how good he had it with us."

1943—Mob extortion rocks Hollywood

In 1943, Hollywood was rocked by an extortion plot operated by Frank Nitti, who had taken over for the imprisoned Al Capone, and Paul Ricca, one of Nitti's underbosses. Nitti and Ricca were connected to many of the Hollywood unions, including the stage handlers and movie projectionists unions.

In this capacity, Nitti and Ricca were able to extort hundreds of thousands of dollars from the major Hollywood studios, such as MGM, 20th Century-Fox, RKO, and Paramount. Money was collected by threat of lighting Bette Davis too well, splicing clips from the first Tweety Bird cartoon ("A Tale of Two Kitties") into prints of *The Flying Tigers*, and locking Errol Flynn in his trailer and towing it to a Catholic girls school.

The only time Nitti and Ricca slipped up was when they threatened RKO that projectionists might "accidentally" show a re-edited version of *The Magnificent Ambersons* that was only 12 minutes long. RKO approved the cut and gave Nitti and Ricca co-producer credits.

1974—The Watergate tapes

Recent technological advances have allowed analysts to piece together this segment of the missing eighteen-and-a-half minutes of the Watergates tapes. This exchange includes what many believe to be an extortion attempt against President Nixon.

(*Historical note:* Despondent over the fact that *The Bob Newhart Show* was in summer reruns, Nixon had recently dug up his copy of *The Button-Down Mind Strikes Back*, and had thereby gotten the idea to disconnect the recording device in his phone. As a result, we are left with only his half of this conversation.)

NIXON: Hello, Bill! How's every little thing?

Me? Can't complain. Listen, I'm having Haldeman in here in a while, and—Yeah, he still walks like that. . . . Uh-huh, I know what you mean. Look, Rose Mary said this was urgent, so what's up?

Really? Get any sun?

I see. How'd the fights treat you?

Well, all I know is you don't bet on the white guy. Lose much?

Oh, well, that's too bad. Still, plenty more where that came from, right?

Oh. I didn't realize. Is your mother feeling better?

Oh. Yes, now I remember. Pat sent you a card or something, didn't she?

I'll tell her. But anyway . . .

Really. They said that?

(Expletive deleted), Bill, I told you not to get involved with Cubans. Can't trust them, I said—

Of course, I'm happy to float you a loan, just until things pick up for you. How much?

Christ, Bill, I haven't got that kind of money!

No, I put it all in real estate.

I'm not lying.

Bill, even if I had a million dollars, do you really think I'm going to use it to bail you out of your gambling debts?

What do you mean, "hush money"?

What do you know about that?

The *(expletive deleted)* you do! I carried your ass out of Justice and onto the Court months ago! There's no way you could—

Oh, I see how it is. This is loyalty, is it? Well, let me remind you who you're dealing with, pal. I'm Richard *(expletive deleted)* Nixon, and I'm the President of the United *(expletive deleted)* States of America! I'm not gonna be pushed around, do you hear me?

No, no . . . I'm sorry I got all worked up.

No, it's not you. It's my anniversary tomorrow, and I haven't gotten Pat anything yet, and—

Oh, hey, that is a good idea. I'll send Dean out to pick one up when he goes for lunch.

No, he won't mind. Anyway, about this money problem, try talking to the head of the RNC.

No, the wimp. Whathisname. Old CIA man.

Is that his name? Christ, I have to get a Rolodex or something. Anyway, he's got a pile of money from his oil business, and his son's a coke fiend. You should be able to squeeze him for a million.

That's between him and you, Bill. I don't know, maybe you'll pay him back some day.

That's all right. Just don't forget who your friends are, all right?

That's right. And let me know when you're gonna see those Cubans again. I need more cigars. Kennedy sure *(expletive deleted)* ruined things for the rest of us.

Yeah, I know. And right here in the Oval Office. Some people have no respect, I'm telling you.

[Excerpt ends.]

1985—The Huxtable daughter

In 1985, prominent African-American obstetrician Heathcliff Huxtable received correspondence from a young woman named Sandra Ayers-Allen, in which she claimed to be his illegitimate oldest daughter. Rather than demanding money, Ayers-Allen insisted on being adopted into the Huxtable family, and being treated as though she had always been there.

This included, but was not limited to, attendance at family functions, subsidy of her Princeton education, and later, having the family test products to be sold at her and her husband's wilderness store.

Huxtable acquiesced, fearing that a scandal would have a negative impact on his medical practice and his wife's legal career. Sandra was assimilated into the family and officially became one of the Huxtable kids. In legal circles, this type of extortion has become known as a "reverse Chuck Cunningham," in which an oldest child is paid a sum of money to disappear completely while the rest of the family pretends that he never existed.

SAVE TOBY! 39

1980s–God threatens Oral Roberts

In the mid-eighties, Christian evangelist Oral Roberts was the victim of two extortion attempts involving threats against his life. According to Roberts, in 1985 he was contacted by a deity who identified himself as "God," and was told that unless he (Roberts) raised $8 million, "God" would "call him home." Roberts told police that he understood this term to mean that "God" would kill him.

As a humble minister, Roberts did not have access to that kind of money and was forced to ask his congregation to contribute. The money was raised, and Roberts' life was spared. Apparently, knowing a good thing when he saw it, "God" struck again in 1986, demanding that another $8 million be raised, giving a deadline of March 31. Once again, under threat of "calling home" Roberts.

Roberts swallowed his pride and asked his followers to donate, and without the last minute donation of $1.5 million from a Florida dog track owner, Roberts' life might well have been forfeit.

Authorities have attempted to bring the amoral extortionist known as "God" to justice, but so far have been unable to find an officer willing to serve "God" with a subpoena. "God" is still at large and considered dangerous.

Great Failures in Saving Things

ATTEMPTING TO SAVE SOMETHING IS NOTHING NEW. Many efforts succeed—the save the whales movement of the '80s is a perfect example. You don't hear anything about it anymore. Mission accomplished.

Unfortunately, not every effort has the kind of personnel that Save the Whales, or even we at Save Toby! have. Inevitably, if your plan isn't solid or you fail to get the word out, whatever you are trying to save is doomed.

Here we share some examples of just that kind of mismanagement. These are only a few of the attempts by good Samaritans like us that failed.

SAVE THIS VIETCONG GUY!

Vietnamese people are small and cute, and they are definitely worth saving—and that goes for both sides of the 38th parallel. February 1, 1968, South Vietnam's police chief, Lt. Col. Nguyen Ngoc Loan, started a campaign called Save This Vietcong Guy! on the streets of Saigon's Chinese quarter. The campaign demanded $50 US in order to save an unknown Vietcong prisoner. Photographer Eddie Adams didn't have $50 US to give the colonel, but he did have his camera, and boy, did he earn his dinner that day (plus a Pulitzer)! It is on record as the shortest attempt to save something ever, lasting only 3.2 seconds.

SAVE THE CHICAGOANS!

People from Chicago are so cute when they pout about the Cubs, it makes us all warm and fuzzy inside. Whether they're eating bratwursts or deep-dish pizza, they are always chubby and adorable. In 1919, Al Capone knew what to do: Save the Chicagoans! In exchange for just five dollars a month each, Al Capone promised Chicagoans that no one would throw a brick through their window, burn down their house, or shoot them at night. Some Chicagoans were saved, but some didn't give Capone any money, and so he couldn't save them.

SAVE ANNIE THE PROSTITUTE!

Prostitutes are pretty and nice, especially if they have a heart of gold, like Julia Roberts in the all-time favorite, *Pretty Woman*. In 1888, Jack the Ripper started the Save Annie the Prostitute! campaign with the hopes of saving London streetwaker Annie Chapman, who was both really poor and really cute. He started working to save Annie at 2 a.m. on September seventh, and worked hard to save her until 10 a.m. Annie wasn't saved, but not for lack of trying. Remarkably, Jack's truly prolific attempts to save things were met only with failure ever to do so successfully.

SAVE A SERF!

The Middle Ages sucked in a lot of ways, but everyone loved the serfs. They wore little caps, floppy shoes, and had big eyes on one side of their head. In 820 AD, feudal Lord Peppin began the Save a Serf! campaign, where he tried to save the life of his property, a man named Bodo. The campaign started when Bodo was born in a muddy ditch.

Peppin said that he would save Bodo in return for the lifelong servitude of the other one hundred people living on his land. Bodo's

townsfolk worked very hard, but not hard enough to save Bodo. So Peppin took Bodo's clothes and bread. Bodo died of a cold when he was 29. The 29 years of saving Bodo is the longest campaign to save something that we've ever heard of.

THE ORIGIN OF SAVE TOBY!

Note: The following is based loosely on events that never took place, but *had* they occurred . . . this is more than likely what would have happened, possibly.

JAMES: I suited up in my standard jogging attire and walked out of the back door for a quick stretch before my morning run. The summer mornings that I took for granted had come to a close, and fall became an all too familiar setting. Leaves from the massive oak and cypress trees covered my backyard.

The wind howled; I breathed in the cold air through my nose. The sun rose across the lake, a giant lasso roping in the darkness of dawn like a black Angus. Throwing my left leg onto the railing of my hardwood deck, squinting in pain, I closed my eyes and pulled my torso toward my knee. I could feel the slow tear of muscle fibers. Six, seven, eight, I pulled back and the pain subsided. I heard a rattling of leaves on the ground, but didn't think much of it. I switched legs, and I reached out to grab my right ankle. Only this time, I did not close my eyes—instead, they became fixed on something.

There, below my porch, in an otherwise dark place blanketed with earth and withered leaves, sat a stunning creature. The sun shone through the trees and dappled this tiny baby bunny with light. As our eyes met, he began to shake. Seemingly abandoned and wounded, he was nestled beneath the leaves with only his tiny head poking through. Cautiously, I knelt beside him. Using my hands, I 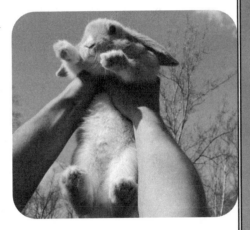 gently scooped him up and raised him up to the sky. He trembled and looked into my eyes, terrified. The wind whispered to me, *His name shall be Loby*. "That's ridiculous," I said to the wind, "I'm going to call him Toby instead . . . *bitch*." I stroked his tangled and tattered mane to assure him everything was okay.

I brought Toby into the warmth of my home. I took a soft white towel from the linen closet and laid it out on the wood floor of my den. I placed Toby on the towel and placed a bowl of water next to him. I only wished that I could convince him that every-thing would be all right. After a few minutes, his trembling subsided.

Tentatively, Toby began to take his first steps after his rescue. As he hobbled to the water bowl, I immediately noticed an injury  to his right hind leg. He dragged it on the carpet as he moved around, and I also noticed a little blood on the white towel. I let him drink from the water for a minute, then I took it away when he was finished. I wrapped him up in the towel for warmth and to prevent further injury to his hind leg, and I proceeded directly to the nearest veterinarian.

Luckily, the vet's office opened shortly after our arrival. The doc said Toby had been injured by a sharp object, most likely the claw of an animal. The puncture wound was deep; the claw had ripped through his skin and sliced one of his tendons, rendering Toby's right leg nearly unusable. Unfortunately, Toby's small size made the wound inoperable. Only time could heal it.

On the way home, I stopped by the store and picked up everything I would need to care for Toby. When we arrived back home, I set up a place for Toby to live within my den. I fenced off a small section of floor, laid out some pine bedding, and placed down a small cloth mat for Toby to sleep on. I provided a log of wood and a tennis ball for him to push around. As it neared five o'clock, I knew that my roommate, Brian, would soon be home. I felt anxious about how Brian would take the addition of my new friend, our new roommate.

BRIAN: I got home about five thirty. Traffic sucked, and I was pissed. The boss had been busting my chops all day long. On top of that, he said we had some extra shipments going out this quarter, and he said, "If you don't come in on Saturday, then don't bother coming in on Sunday!" Son of a bitch. The only thing I wanted was to get my hands on a cold brew, but as soon as I opened the door, what I got was the pungent slap of animal stink. It made me furious. "James!" I called out, "what the hell is that smell? What fury have you unleashed in our bathroom?" As I walked into the den, I noticed some sort of enclosure set up on the floor. The smell was thick and unbearable, and I beheld some kind of rodent creature. James quickly came in and explained what had transpired earlier in the day. He started some cracked-out spiel about how he had found this little nugget and made friends. *What a bunch of crap*, I thought. I told him straight up that there was no way that we were going to keep this little stink bomb. I cringed at the thought of bringing some lady friend home to this smell. However, James remained adamant that his new "friend" stay in our house for a while. Knowing that James had very few friends, I conceded to let the little beast stay—but only until he recovered.

JAMES: Over the next few weeks, I spent nearly every waking moment by Toby's side. I focused my attention on making his recovery process as smooth as possible, providing comfort and nourishment. During those weeks, I helped Toby clean his wounds, both physical and emotional. All the while, we forged a mutual bond of friendship, as well as an understanding that I would always be there to watch over him. I resolved to do everything in my power to give Toby the best life possible. Over several weeks of valiant effort, Toby regained his strength. Toby's a fighter, that's for sure.

About six weeks later, Toby had almost fully recovered. His progress was astonishing. His wounds had fully healed, and he had regained the ability to run around. The only reminders of the attack were several large scars running down his leg. His appetite recovered as fast as his injuries. One evening, I sat down next to him with a plate of carrots, his favorite dish. Brian had built a fire earlier that evening, and we enjoyed its warmth as we ate. As the flames consumed the logs, I took a seat in our favorite chair and set him down in front of the hearth, so he could play in its warmth. I reached for a bowl of fresh fruits and spring water that I had prepared for his dessert. Dessert was always a special treat

for Toby, and I could tell how much he appreciated it. After finishing his meal he gazed up at me with a look of gratitude and understanding. As Toby turned his head and gazed into the flames, I could see the valor in his eyes. Toby was no longer haunted by fear of the outside world. He sat tall, and he had the stoic look of inner confidence. As Toby turned to me, he began to hop and dance with joy and excitement like a member of Riverdance, or maybe even Stomp— those guys kick ass. With every leap, I could see him embracing the prospects of the future.

Later that night, I lay in bed and reflected on the events of the eve- ning. My relationship with Toby had reached a new level. Toby and I had become more than just companions, we were truly friends. It was at this moment that I realized Toby loved me.

BRIAN: James had become more and more distant over those few weeks. When I sat out on the porch smoking a fat stogy after work, I sat alone. James was retreating into isolation from me and the outside world. The attention he gave that rabbit was bordering on obsessive. In the past, I was accustomed to coming home and tossing around a pigskin or setting off a few fireworks, but James began to protest these activities. Apparently, little King Toby got upset by the noise of cherry bombs and black cats. The cigar smoke wasn't good for his little lungs, so no more smoking in the house. I began to question whether this was my own house or a concentration camp run by a tiny dictator.

On one cold, winter Friday night, I saw how James truly felt for that animal. Like every week, I wanted to cook up a fat, thick, juicy steak as a Friday reward for having completed my workweek. I like my meat cooked the way real men do it—over wood coals—

and the metal grate in our fireplace makes it an ideal grill.

The sound of the steak sizzling was like music to my ears. Our whole home filled with the aroma of the beef, and for once it didn't stink of James's rabbit. As I flipped my steak, I could not ignore the somewhat disturbing thought that came over me. *Grilled rabbit is quite succulent, and having lived most of its life indoors, our little pet probably wouldn't have the gamey taste of most wild rabbits.* Although I would have no qualms throwing that little nugget on the coals, I knew I could never do that to James. I quickly put the idea out of my mind.

Nothing goes better with steak and potatoes than a cold beer and good cigar. I decided to eat out on the porch where I could enjoy both without having to worry about "upsetting the bunny." As I savored every morsel of the steak, my eyes wandered back into the house. Sitting outside in the dark, I was invisible to James as he stoked the fire in the living room. I could see him cuddling that filthy creature like a mother with a newborn child. It was a bizarre situation, and I was fascinated by just how weird my roommate had become. James just sat there, mesmerized by this

rabbit, staring into the flames. The rabbit was clearly happy to be close to the fire, but had a glazed look in his beady little eyes.

I killed my first beer and was glad that I had thought ahead to bring out a second one.

If I had known what was going to happen next, I definitely would not have taken such a big swig out of the freshly opened bottle. It seemed that dumb little Toby became a little too ambitious and got right up to the fire. As one of the logs settled, a shower of small sparks flew from the fireplace. As each one came in contact with him, he leapt in the air. It reminded me of a Wild West cowboy shooting bullets at someone's feet and shouting, "Dance! Dance!" The sight was too much for me, the beer came spewing out my nose, and I fell out of my chair laughing hysterically. That damn bunny jumping around in the air made my whole weekend.

JAMES: Still groggy as I stumbled into the kitchen for my morning cup of coffee, I glanced over to Toby's pen and noticed he was missing. I knelt down to see if he had gone to his usual hiding spot in the back of the pen. He was gone.

"Toby!" I called out, but saw nothing. Frantically, I ran from room to room in search of my little friend. To my dismay, he was nowhere in the house. I ventured outside, and as I stepped onto the porch, I saw Toby frolicking in the yard, which instantly

relieved my fears. As I stepped down into the yard to embrace my little buddy, I saw a flash in the corner of my eye. I whipped my head up just in time to catch a glimpse of a large, gruesome beast swooping down from the sky, right toward Toby!

I leapt into action. I sprinted toward Toby and dove through the air, my hands just missing his tiny body as a massive bald eagle snatched him up with huge jagged talons. The bird of prey swept Toby skyward like a twin engine Cessna or a fire-breathing Tomahawk missile from the '80s. Helplessly, I watched as the eagle took Toby to his nest, high atop a cypress tree. The predator stared down at me with a look of triumph. Overwhelmed with agony, I dropped to my knees and cried out in anguish.

With tears running down my cheeks, I lifted my head with all the strength I could muster. Through my tear-blurred eyes I caught a glimpse of light from across the lake. I strained to focus on the light. What I had originally mistaken for a single flash was actually a vast array of small flickers. I ran down to the shore desperate to find help. Once I reached the water's edge, I saw that the flickers originated from the stretched out arms of thousands of people who each held a silver rung of a gigantic ladder. I screamed at the top of my lugs, "HELP, PLEASE HELP!" My screams were drowned in the waves and could not be heard by those across the lake. Once again, I became filled with agony. Across the lake was the key to Toby's salvation, yet I remained powerless.

BEEP:BEEP:BEEP. Red lights flashing, six thirty a.m. I leapt from my bed, startled by the clamor of the alarm and the events of my dream.

BRIAN: I lay down on the futon and threw on some late-night television. *A funny night*, I thought to myself as I relaxed with a beer balancing on my gut. Still, I felt uneasy about the transformation I'd witnessed in James over the past few weeks. Moreover, the thought of eating the bunny—which occurred to me earlier, while grilling my steak—lingered in the back of my mind. *Should I feel guilty because it's James's "friend"?* The little dumpling had grown into a sizeable meal in a matter of weeks. It didn't matter. I was drunk, so I passed out.

The next evening, I got back from work as normal, but James's car wasn't in the driveway. I walked into the house, thirsty as hell and ready to relax, because once again, the boss had been bustin' my chops. I went to the fridge. *Looks like James spent the beer money on Toby and these damn Zimas. Awesome,* I thought, *guess I'll have to drink one of those.* I cracked open the bottle and put the cold liquid to my lips. *Disgusting, this tastes the way Toby smells, no wonder James likes it.* As I chugged the last of it, I could hear my empty stomach rumbling. I opened the freezer to thaw out some steaks. Nothing there. I must have forgotten to buy extra tender-loins this week. I checked the fridge, but all I found was carrots and celery. *Toby, you've screwed me for the last time.*

I ran over to Toby's pen and snatched him up. "You've gotten big," I said to the little guy. His legs dangled and he began to squirm in my hand. His back legs clawed at my wrist, but I held firm. Placing him on the cutting board with one hand and grab-bing my Ginsu knife with the other (*Now what would you pay?*), he flopped around like a fish. As he clawed at the countertop with all his might, I easily subdued him with one hand. I was ecstatic at the thought of this great meal and the idea of ridding the putrid-smelling creature from my life. I raised my right arm high and brought it down like a hammer. With the strength of a grizzly, and the wisdom of a man, I lopped off his head with a

single stroke. Blood spewed onto my shirt and across the kitchen counter. I laughed as his head rolled along the table and his body went lifeless. *I'm going to have some good eatin' tonight,* I thought.

I carefully cleaned and quartered the carcass. *A bit of Tobyswick Stew* will really hit the spot,* I thought. I envisioned the dish at its completion: the warm broth, the chunks of Toby filling my stomach. I prepared the meal carefully, paying special attention to the recipe. As I finally sat down to enjoy my feast, I felt at ease with the world. The terrible creature that had been dragging James into the depths of madness had finally been eliminated. I reached down deep into the bowl and scooped up the biggest chunk of Toby out of the pot. The aroma captivated my senses. As I brought the chunk of meat to my mouth, my nostrils flared and

*See recipe, page 109.

I began to salivate. I opened my mouth wide, stuffed the spoonful into my mouth, and chewed with gusto.

As I awoke from my dream, I was soaked with sweat from being near the fire. *I must have gotten really drunk*, I thought. A thunderous hangover pained my head. I looked at Toby, who lay asleep on the floor in his pen. As I stared at the little animal, I was torn between relief and sadness.

JAMES: After a long day filled with disappointing news at the factory, I was excited to see Toby. I jingled the keys at the door to let Toby know I had arrived. Unfortunately, because of recent payroll cutbacks at the plant, I had to stop buying fresh vegetables for Toby. Money was getting really tight for us, but all I wanted was to make Toby the happiest bunny in the world. In order to make it up to him, I decided to build him an incredible new toy companion. I popped in my favorite Kenny G disc to help get the creative juices flowing. I spent several hours that night building an elaborate toy out of a pinecone and various craft supplies. I constructed the arms and legs out of Popsicle sticks, colorful pipe cleaners, and googly eyes. I attached a papier-mâché face to complete Toby's new companion. After finishing the gift, I was too tired to present it to him that evening. I hit the sack, and it was only a matter of moments before I was sound asleep.

After my usual morning jog, I was eager to show Toby the toy that had taken me the better part of the evening to create. I walked into the kitchen, still soaking wet from my morning run, and grabbed the toy. I took it over to his pen and carefully laid the pinecone companion down on the floor. Toby perked up at the sight of this new foreign object. After a few seconds of inspection, Toby walked over to the opposite side of the pen with a look of disinterest. Each step away from the toy that he took punctured my heart like a thousand flaming swords of Arabia or shots from an AK-47 assault rifle shooting at maximum speed and capacity. Needless to say, I was upset. Still puzzled from Toby's reaction, I decided to leave for work. Maybe he would grow to like his toy over time.

I spent the entire day at the office hoping that Toby was at home learning to better enjoy his new gift. I bounded up the steps and opened the front door. I quickly ran over to his pen, but I was not prepared for what I saw. Toby had devoured the gift. I stared at the tattered pieces of the toy that lay strewn about the pen. Toby glared at me. I ran into my bedroom. What had I done to upset Toby? I resolved to do anything in my power to make Toby as happy as possible and live the life he truly deserved.

The next day, on my weekly trip to the local pet supply store, I stumbled upon what seemed to be a solution to my problem. As I

walked into the shop, something immediately caught my eye. On the front counter, inside of a small glass case, sat a strikingly shiny object. Shaped like a small cylindrical cage, the toy had two large wheels on each end with columns connecting them. Both the wheels and columns had obviously been hand painted with great care and precision. Intertwined colors and designs wrapped seamlessly around the toy. The tag indicated that the colors had been chosen specially to please the taste of a rabbit; however, any creature could clearly see its beauty. The cage contained a single crystalline sphere, which in turn contained several small golden beads. The sound it produced resembled a million tiny raindrops falling on an endless pane of glass in the summer. At this moment, I knew that this toy had been created solely for Toby, the greatest bunny of all time and maybe even the greatest in all the animal kingdom, or phyla.

In life, nothing good comes easily. I would have to make tremendous sacrifices over the next few weeks. However, I was more than willing to give up a large portion of my salary to see happiness in Toby's eyes.

I purchased the toy and made my way home in eager anticipation of Toby's reaction. After what seemed like forever, I arrived, ready to present the gift to Toby. With the gift still wrapped, I sat down next to him in the pen. I carefully unwrapped the toy and removed it from its wooden case. Toby's head perked up to see what I held out for him. As he caught a glimpse of the treasure, Toby hopped over to it in elation. He launched the toy into the air, and with a second leap, he caught the toy in his mouth. Our eyes met, and time froze. I realized for the first time that Toby's prior feelings of anger and displeasure were born out of a thirst for more. Toby needed to live life like a king.

BRIAN: The situation quickly got worse. James was going nuts, quite possibly bananas. The first sign slapped me like a wheel of cheese as I walked into the house and Kenny G

was blaring. I knew something was up. I walked into James's room, and he was giggling like a schoolgirl about creating some home-made toy for Toby. When Toby didn't even look twice at the toy, the expression on James's face was hilarious. The icing on the cake was when Toby ate half of the thing, and James thought it was because the little rabbit was upset with him. I tried to tell him, "It's just a rabbit. That's what they do, they eat things," but he just lowered his head and walked out of the room. I couldn't help but feel sorry for the guy. There was something special about this rabbit, though. James had been feeding Toby nothing but high-carb foods. His belly grew big, his thighs were plump. Every day I sat and watched the bunny get bigger, I waited and waited for the right time.

One day, James rolled in with a decorated box, a "gift for Toby." I watched as he placed the toy in Toby's pen. The dumb rabbit had no clue what was going on. He just jumped around a bit, and as soon as James left, he started peeing all over the toy. I moved in to get a better view, and the toy looked like a fine piece of jewelry, not something meant for a rabbit. Later that night, I talked with James, and he said we had to cut back on our expenses, like cable, on account of Toby's refined tastes. I was speechless. Awestruck by his stupidity, I turned away from James and ran out of the room and straight to my computer. I knew what had to be done.

I'd been brainstorming for weeks, but when the idea came, it was in the form of a dream. A dream that I knew could come true. I wanted Toby either to die or never to interfere in my life again. If we could raise enough money, we could live separate lives. Toby could be cared for in a different section of the house, one that had all the niceties that James wanted him to have. If we couldn't raise that money, I would be forced to eat him—I'm not giving up cable. The only fitting solution was to let a third party decide Toby's fate. The Internet was the only viable alternative. When I had finished my project later that week, I told James what I had done.

"James, get in here, I've got something to tell you."

"What is it?"

"Toby has been ruining this household for months. He's created nothing but problems for the both of us, and it's time for them to be resolved."

"What are you talking about? Toby has been nothing but a blessing to us, he's my best friend and I love the little guy."

"Listen to yourself. He's not your best friend, he's a rabbit. You see everything he does in some twisted way. When he ate the toy, you thought he was upset. When he jumped around after seeing that ridiculous thing you bought, you thought he was happy."

"NO! He was happy! I know it!"

"You're being ridiculous, it's like you've gone mad or something, and I'm not going to let it ruin my life! You've left me no choice. When you leave the house, I'm going to cook that little nugget into a nice, juicy rabbit steak."

serious ending

"This doesn't make any sense, Brian. Why would you do that now?"

"That's the thing, James, I'm not going to eat him now. The public will decide his fate. I've made savetoby.com, a website whose proceeds will go to funding a new wing for Toby to live in. However, the only way to attract public interest is to have his death be a real possibility."

"I need Toby to be a part of me forever. If he has to die, then I will be the one to eat him."

"I don't care who eats him, as long as he's out of my life somehow."

"So how will the public save him?"

"Well, the website must raise sufficient funds so that Toby can live away from me in a life that you want for him. There's even a book deal in the making."

"So be it," said James.

alternate ending #1

"And I'm the one who's crazy? There's no way I'm going to let you eat my rabbit!"

"Well, luckily, I've come up with the perfect plan" I said.

"What are you talking about?"

"The public will decide Toby's fate, by buying this book in which we've been fictitiously created."

"Neat," James said and disappeared in a puff of logic.

"I know!" I said, dissolving in an explosion of laughter, "HAHAHAHA! All will crumble under savetoby.com!"

alternate ending #2

"And I'm the one who's crazy? If you kill him, I'll die inside! If anyone consumes Toby, it must be me!" James replied.

"I knew you'd say that. I've got the solution to all of our problems."

"WHAT IS IT?!" James asked.

"SAVETOBY.COM!" I stomped my feet and clapped my hands.

"A website?" He began to break dance as he asked the question.

"Yes, just ch-ch-ch-check it out now!" I scribbled on an imaginary turntable and finished by doing the robot.

alternate ending #3

"Don't even think about it!" James replied.

"Oh, I've thought about it, I'm thinking about it right now!"

"Oh no you didn't!" James said, snapping his fingers.

I reached in to the pocket of my sagging pants, past the crack rocks and to the right of my pager. I pulled out my nine and pointed it at his head. "It's about to get real wet in here, son."

James suddenly reached down into his jeans with both hands and pulled out a sawed-off shotgun and a 40 oz. "I'm about to split yo brain, son!" he said while tipping back the 40.

"If you want beef, here's beef!"

Gunshots erupted, and they both fell to the ground dead. Toby hopped up on James, and pooped.

Letters from Toby

I ALWAYS THOUGHT THAT THE MORE PERSONAL we could make the relationship between Toby and the general public, the more compelling his story would be and the more likely we would be to reach our goal. The truth is, we don't want to eat Toby. We'd rather have burgers and fries, but a deal is a deal.

In the beginning, we tried to gauge Toby's mood and keep a diary of how he seemed to feel as we told him the plan and counted down the days. The problem is, Toby always has the same look on his face. It's hard to read a rabbit.

Then one day, I was watching TBS and *The Horse Whisperer* came on. It's not Robert Redford's best work, but it gave me an idea. I

made some phone calls, and eventually found a rabbit whisperer.

She agreed to transcribe Toby's thoughts for us in exchange for 5 percent of the profits of his book. We talked her down to a bag of old clothes and a carton of Kools.

Once she explained the situation to Toby, he refused to participate in our diary idea. Instead, he insisted on dictating letters to his bunny friends. Here are Toby's letters.

March 1, 2005

Friends,

Well, you probably heard already—I've been kidnapped. Technically, I suppose I've been bunnynapped, but I'm not writing argue semantics. I just want you all to know I'm okay. All and all, my captors are pretty nice so far. See, I got jacked up good by this alley cat and crawled under this porch. Then these guys rescued me and took me inside. They cleaned me up, fed me, and took a bunch of pictures. I'm not sure what they want or how long I'll be here just yet, but it's not so bad. Tell everyone I said hi, and I'll see you all soon, okay?

Take it easy,
Toby

March 9, 2005

Amigos,

It's been a few days now and I just wanted to let you all know I'm still okay. My wounds are all healed and they're feeding me *really* well! It's almost like they're trying to fatten me up or something, but no matter. I can just get back on my usual cardio program when I get back home, and I'll be back

in shape in no time. Anyhow, that's about it for now. I miss everyone and I can't wait to get back!

Stay cool
The Tobinator

March 17, 2005

Hey gang

I'm hoping to be released any day now. Things are good and I'm holding up. This isn't all that different from that time two years ago when I was in for drug trafficking. Just waiting the days out, although in this case, it doesn't involve the murder of a key witness. Anyhow, I should be seeing you all real soon.

Keep it real,
T-Bone

March 25, 2005

To anyone reading this,

Help me, please. This isn't what I thought. These guys, my captors, they're getting all crazy on me. Yesterday they got me all primped up for a photo—in a cooking pot! Then they took one of me on a cutting board. I'm seriously worried that these guys are going to eat me. So please, rescue me. I'll write again when I know more.

Freaking out,
Tobe

April 5, 2005

To my people,

So here's the deal. I'm being held for some kind of ransom. I'm not sure of the details, but let's just say it's a hefty sum. So I am calling on you animal lovers out there, please step up and help a bunny out. They're going to kill me, cook me, and eat me. We can't have that. Look at me, look how cute I am! I can't go out like that. If I'm going to check out early it's got to be in style. Run down by an 18-wheeler like my cousin Lenny or shot with a 12 gauge like my uncle Ashton. But captured and cooked? Please, get some scratch together for my

Hop or chop? You decide!

Toby takes it to the streets.

On the prowl for beach bunnies.

The circle of life.

Log on to www.savetoby.com.

Toby's life's too short not to
smell the flowers—
unless you save him!

Roses are red,
Violets are purple,
Toby is sweet,
And—uh...damn it!

Toby, the greatest bunny of all time and maybe even the greatest in all the animal kingdom, or phyla.

Toby finds arbitrage opportunities in the commodities markets.

That tortoise is going down.

Repping the brand.

Toby or not to be, that is the question.

Toby built his financial
empire brick by brick.

Sittin' on 24 carrots.

The ladies call me "Thumper."

Do they love Toby
or his bunny style?

Where's the cotton-tailgate?

What are you waiting for? Buy the book! Hurry!

cause. Have a bake sale, sell some old shoes on eBay, whatever it is you humans do for extra scratch—and use it to buy copies of *Save Toby!* It's the only way I'm getting out alive.

A homie in need,
Tobe-Loc

April 16, 2005

To whom is concerned,
This rabbit is in some serious droppings. Some of you have ponied up and bought the book, and for that I'm grateful, but I'm worried it ain't enough—not even close. I've never been much of a charity case in the past, and as much as I hate to do it now, I need help. So please do what you can and then some. These guys are going for a big score here, and frankly, I'm afraid they've overestimated my value. Only you can prove me wrong. Won't you prove me wrong? Please?

Begging for the first time
Tow-Bee

April 25, 2005

To the outside world,
Depression has set in. As I sit here on death row, it is becoming painfully obvious that the book is not selling fast enough and I will be eaten by my captors. My only hope is that I can somehow be metabolized into their bodies and haunt them, but that's a long shot. I'm doomed, and I never got to do everything I wanted to. To those of you on the outside, live your life! Live each day as if it were your last, because God knows at any moment you could be captured and eaten.

Let me make one last plea for you buy up copies of *Save Toby!* There's still hope. Maybe Oprah will find out about this. She's somewhat of an animal lover, and doesn't she have a book club?
Suddenly finding religion,

T.

May 17, 2005

Hey everybody,

Would I be better as a stew or a roast? These guys need to know what you think.

Thanks for everything,
Toby

June 4, 2005

You cheap bastards,

We've sold a lot of books, but *some* of you still haven't pitched in! Here I am in my moment of need and you're out there spending your money on strippers and blow. I've been through anger and crippling depression, but I'm slowly working my way toward acceptance. I hope you all haven't accepted my imminent death. I sure haven't. Now get out there, get paid, and get me out of here!

Toby in the News

COPYCATS ABOUND
June 1, 2005

CHARLOTTE, NC—Following the report on *NBC Nightly News* with Brian Williams about the Save Toby! Web site, several newspapers have reported that pet stores nationwide are experiencing a spike in rabbit purchases. It is uncertain whether the trend can be attributed to a renewed interest in rabbits as pets, or the desire to cash in on the latest moneymaking fad on the Internet. Efforts to explain the increased interest in rabbits were met with limited success, but Web-

hosting companies are noticing increased search activity on domain names associated with rabbits.

Matt Heitz, VP of Sales for DaddyGo.com, spoke to Reuters about the recent trend. "My reps started noticing this disturbing development last week. At first we figured it was just a fad, but once our domain registrations started going up, we realized we had a serious cash-making opportunity on our hands." Although Heitz went on record as saying that DaddyGo does not encourage cruelty to animals, off the record he told reporters, "This is a huge deal for us. We're hoping some dumbass threatens to kill a dolphin. Man, that would be the next level! This killing beloved animals thing is going *huge!*"

Pet store owners across the country were similarly enthusiastic about the upswing in rabbit sales that is providing extra revenue to their stagnant business model. Robert Word, owner of Pets Unlimited in Pittsburgh, gushed about the increase in his business. "If it wasn't for those kids threatening to kill Toby, I wouldn't be able to afford my annual vacation to Jacksonville, Florida."

Word is uncertain what the new rabbit owners are planning on doing with their bunnies, and he feels that ignorance is the best policy. "Frankly, I don't give a damn what they do once they take the furry critter home. In fact, I wish I had thought of this ransom idea sooner. Maybe I'd be able to go somewhere really cool like the south Jersey shore."

With the Save Toby! Web site experiencing a spike in traffic since the airing of the story on NBC, an analyst with Yahoo! told reporters that company search engines were noticing an increase in searches on the terms "rabbit," "ransom," and "rabbit recipes." According to the analyst at Yahoo!, "With search traffic like this, it's only a matter of time before some other sicko gets the same idea. We're talking big bucks here for just sitting around and updating a Web site once a day

with some snapshots of a rabbit in a cage. I don't know why I didn't think of this. I have a frigging boatload of credit card debt I need to pay off."

Despite the enthusiastic response to Save Toby!'s success in the business world, animal lovers nationwide were considerably less pleased. Jenny Gilbert, national recruitment director for PETA, was outraged about Toby's plight. "I find it absolutely appalling that in this day and age, some demented lunatic can put up a Web site threatening to kill a poor, harmless rabbit. I have some of my people hot on his trail, and if I find the sick bastard, he'd better watch his back." When asked what she had in mind, Gilbert was coy. "I'm not saying anything about anything, but if I was him, I'd think twice before starting my car in the morning."

At the University of Wisconsin, Gilbert's veiled threats fell on deaf ears when it came to the Phi Omega Omega fraternity. They are reportedly holding a dolphin for ransom and advertising their demands on the Web site www.saveflipper.com.

Although it is unknown whether the fraternity even has possession of an actual dolphin, they have already collected $12,000 from worried dolphin lovers. Social Chairman Brent Metzger told CBS News that the fraternity is planning a Luau-themed party featuring a live dolphin in a shark tank to celebrate the end of the school year. "Dude, this party is gonna be off tha chain. Flipper in the hizzie!"

Upon hearing the news of the dolphin's plight, owners of the Save Toby! Web site were unavailable for comment, but they released a brief statement to the press through the Web site. "We here at SaveToby.com do not condone the recent events in Wisconsin. That being said, we're still short of our goal. And I don't need to remind anyone what that means, come the deadline."

Copycats

The Success of SaveToby.com has inspired many imitators to adopt similar tactics. Here are several examples our staff culled from the Web.

SaveHobie.com

An unnamed resident of Louisiana put up this site claiming that unless he received $50,000, he would kill Jeremy Jackson, the second young actor to play David Hasselhoff's son on the popular TV series *Baywatch*. The site was quickly shut down by the authorities. Brandon Call apparently has airtight alibi.

SaveGlobey.com

This site is committed to the preservation and storage of the original props from *Pee-wee's Playhouse*, many of which have reportedly fallen into disrepair. The site includes photos of the various props and set pieces, and they are rather disturbing. "Chairy," for example, seems to be rather badly stained.

SaveFlowbee.com

Sign this online petition to force the U.S. Patent Office to extend inventor Rick Hunt's patent on the vacuum-attached hair cutting

system that has made all of our lives simpler. Otherwise, the market could easily be flooded with inferior knockoffs with fewer safety features and weak suction.

SaveDobie.com

Despondent over not being asked to contribute to the Special Edition DVD release of *How to Stuff a Wild Bikini*, actor Dwayne Hickman has vowed to put a bullet in his brain unless MGM ponies up $25,000 for his audio commentary on the Sandra Dee–George Hamilton classic *Doctor, You've Got to Be Kidding*. Bob Denver has personally contributed $32 already.

SaveOkeechobee.com

Some entrepreneurial, if unoriginal, Florida State University students threatened to release a retrovirus into the popular south Florida destination Lake Okeechobee. They made two crucial mistakes. First, Lake Okeechobee is run by the Army Corps of Engineers, and second, the post–September 11th attitude toward terrorist attacks is less than lenient. They are now being held in Gitmo as enemy combatants. Reportedly, soldiers flushed an FSU class catalog down the toilet.

SaveTheChildren.org

I came across this site just recently, and even I am appalled. I mean, threatening to kill a rabbit is one thing, but human children?! Jesus Christ! What is this world coming to? If the hate mail we get is any indication, they must get some really nasty letters. You do have to respect their commitment to making money.

RaveToby.com

This site seems to be trying to capitalize on Toby's notoriety by

throwing raves with a bunny theme. It's rather lame. I mean, raves are so ten years ago.

PaveToby.com

This may just be a coincidence, but the residents of Brunswick, Indiana, have started a website to collect donations to repave Toby Lane. Apparently, the road is in a state of disrepair.

SaveTobe.com

Jousuke Sugino, who succeeded in the creation of pure white porcelain in the late eighteenth century, is the originator of Tobe style pottery. Many Japanese people have appreciated Tobe pottery, with its simple indigo design on white porcelain, for more than two hundred years. Unfortunately, the lack of master craftsmen in recent years has seen a real decline in the production of quality Tobe pottery. This site asks not for donations, but rather hopes to increase awareness. If you ask me, that is a terrible business model.

DaveToby.com

This is the "official site" of Dave Toby. Who is Dave Toby? How should I know? All I do know is that since the "S" and "D" are so close together on the keyboard, that bastard has been leaching visitors from us for months. If Toby dies, it will be in no small part due to Dave Toby—he is a heartless bastard.

Panel Discussion

SUPPORT@SAVETOBY.COM: After I first launched the website to save Toby, I was utterly shocked by the copious amount of hate-filled letters I received by my fellow animal lovers around the world. I just can't understand it; I love Toby, that's why I started the site—to save him! Thus, in an attempt to comprehend why people hate me so much, I asked one of my colleagues to organize a panel discussion to flush out my opponents' point of view. Here is the transcript from their conversation.

DR. IZZY BIZZY

RALPH

UNFORTUNATELY,

the Somali was too skinny to be captured on film.

SOMALI

ANIMAL ACTIVIST

MODERATOR

MODERATOR: Welcome, everyone. As you all know, we've gathered here to talk about the issues raised by the controversial website SaveToby.com. Why don't you guys introduce yourselves and then we can get started. Crazy Liberal Hippie Animal Activist, why don't you start?

ANIMAL ACTIVIST: Actually, I prefer to be called a "not-crazy, challenged" Liberal Hippie Animal Activist, and I am an adamant member of the Animal-Saving Society Hating Organic-Life-Ending Structures. We as an organization believe that all animal life is precious, that animals are our friends, and they have feelings just like us. We fight for every animal's right to live his life as he sees fit. We want total animal liberation from the corporate slavery that is the food-medical-entertainment-pet complex. So to get our point across, we firebomb the hell out of places.

Dr. Izzy Bizzy: Hi, I'm doctor Izzy Bizzy, professor emeritus of philosophy at Norwich Community College, and I'm here today to tell this crazy animal nut that her argument is incoherent and riddled with logical flaws. Animals have no inherent moral rights, they only have the rights that we as humans assign to them, and the fact that she values animal life more than human life is absolutely ridiculous.

Animal Activist: Flesh eater! How many innocent lives have you ended to fill your thirst for blood?

Dr. Izzy Bizzy: Meat is a valuable source of nutrition, and it is also quite delectable, why should I not partake in—

Ralph: Hell, yeah, meat tastes good! Woooo!

Moderator: Ralph, since you seem so eager to speak, why don't you introduce yourself to the group?

Ralph: Sup, I'm Ralph, but all my Delta Kap bros all call me T.B., it's short for turd buster . . . hah, you know . . . 'cause I love me some meat . . . dude, that Toby joint is hilarious, yeah . . . Norwich C.C. rules! . . . Hey, um, what's with stickman in the corner? . . . he's been mad-eying me since we got here. Hey, you! Yo, what you looking at, cause it's not cool, man, you got something to say? Cause you better just back up, dude.

Starving Somali: Yeah, um, sorry. I just wandered in here because I thought there was going to be a free lunch . . . uuungh, so hungry . . .

Moderator: Great, now that we're all acquainted, who would like to start?

Dr. Izzy Bizzy: See! You activist fool, look at this starving boy. How can you think "liberating" animals is more important than allowing this poor child to eat a hamburger?

ANIMAL ACTIVIST: Why should a cow have to die just to save his life? We don't have to kill things because we want to eat! He should just grab a double-tall, extra-soy, no-stem wheatgrass shake with a side of falafel; not the bleeding flesh of my bovine friend.

RALPH: Wait, wha? You drink grass? Dude, I had to do that as a pledge one time, hah, saw some sweet green nuggets when I booted after the party.

DR. IZZY BIZZY: That is an absurd argument, of course things have to die if we are going to eat. You're killing the grass, as well as the soy and garbanzo plants aren't you?

ANIMAL ACTIVIST: No, Bizzy, you're totally wrong, with new organic farming methods, we can harvest from these plants without killing them. It is important to live in harmony and balance with the life force of all living things. And besides, they're plants, and animals are more important than stupid plants.

STARVING SOMALI: Just . . . any kind of food . . . please. . . . Look at my ribs. . . .

DR. IZZY BIZZY: Well then, how can you refute my assertion that humans are more important than "stupid" animals? Even if we agree that animal life is "valuable," we have to agree as a general principle that human life takes precedence over the lives of animals.

ANIMAL ACTIVIST: Yeah, but what really defines a "human being"? Are we supposed to keep this general standard for brain-dead vegetables on life support, huh? You know, if people keep eating genetically enhanced meat products, more and more people will have serious health problems. And then what? What is our society going to do with all the vegetables that take up valuable hospital space?

RALPH: Blend 'em into hippie-ass veggie shakes! Serve them with some couscous!

DR. IZZY BIZZY: I'm just trying to establish a general principle here, not argue semantics. Do you consider yourself to be a human being?

ANIMAL ACTIVIST: Of course.

DR. IZZY BIZZY: Do you think that animal life is more valuable than your own life?

ANIMAL ACTIVIST: I've dedicated my whole life to saving animals . . . so yes, I guess you could say that I value animals more than myself. It's called self-sacrifice, my friend, one of the steps toward spiritual enlightenment.

DR. IZZY BIZZY: Well, then, by your logic, you should exercise this "self-sacrifice" and go feed yourself to a hungry grizzly. Think of the hundreds of more valuable salmon lives you'll save. But instead, you refuse to go away, and our society has to pay for your stay in prison every time you get arrested because of your incessant protests, which ends up costing us double the amount typically needed to pay for general life support in a hospital!

RALPH: Hah, word! Hypocrite!

ANIMAL ACTIVIST: No, no, no, I don't think I'm a hypocrite at all. These animals need me to stay alive so I can fight for their rights. They need someone who can stand up to you flesh-eating oppressors. I'm just like all the other important freedom fighters. And I'm proud of the fact that I've been arrested twelve times for my protests; it means that people are taking notice of our movement. I'm just following in the footsteps of other "routine lawbreakers" like Dr. Martin Luther King Jr., Mahatma Gandhi, and Jesus.

save toby! 77

RALPH: Whoa, did she just compare herself to Jesus?

STARVING SOMALI: The missionaries in my country told me I would never thirst or hunger again if I ate this Jesus guy, but all they gave me was a cracker and a thimble of grape juice. . . . I'm so hungry. . . .

DR. IZZY BIZZY: How dare you compare yourself to those leaders! You burn down laboratories and routinely practice acts of violence in the interest of your so-called "animal liberation."

ANIMAL ACTIVIST: Yes, that's true; we have been known to *free* animals from the cages of cruel medical experiments, and afterwards we make sure that such evil never continues by destroying the *torture* lab. Can't you see that our use of violence is not a moral issue, but rather it is an effective tactic to fight for the good of animal rights?

DR. IZZY BIZZY: I thought you said that being "ethical" was part of your organization's mission?

ANIMAL ACTIVIST: No, no, you're thinking of a different group. I'm a member of the Animal-Saving Society Hating Organic-Life-Ending Structures.

MODERATOR: Oh . . . Damn, I got the wrong animal activist, I just saw the acronym and figured it was the right group. Oh, well, this organization seems to be pretty much the same as the one I was looking for.

DR. IZZY BIZZY: Wait a minute, let me get this straight. You are completely opposed to medical experimentation on animals, right?

ANIMAL ACTIVIST: Yes, with all my spiritual being.

DR. IZZY BIZZY: Isn't that a diabetes medical alert bracelet on your wrist?

ANIMAL ACTIVIST: So what?

DR. IZZY BIZZY: You do know that the insulin you take was derived from animal testing, right?

ANIMAL ACTIVIST: Well, like I said before, I need to live so I can help fight for these animals' rights.

DR. IZZY BIZZY: So you think animal testing is necessary . . . so that you can stay alive . . . so that you can fight against animal testing?

ANIMAL ACTIVIST: Yeah, that's right.

DR. IZZY BIZZY: Hah, wow. The ridiculous circular flaw in your reasoning shows that either you are incredibly stupid or you want to live more than you want to truly defend your cause . . . and perhaps both.

STARVING SOMALI: I want to live. . . .

ANIMAL ACTIVIST: Can't you see that I *need* to live so that people like *him* (points to Somali) don't resort to killing innocent animal lives to feed their blood lust? You just love eating meat, don't you. If you could, you would even eat an endangered species, wouldn't you.

STARVING SOMALI: Huh? Of course, I would. . . . I already ate my shoe.

ANIMAL ACTIVIST: See! That's what I'm talking about! Somebody needs to stop these tyrannical poachers before all our precious animal friends are lost.

RALPH: I ate a shoe one time . . . damn, that night was crazy.

DR. IZZY BIZZY: You can't honestly believe that animals are actually your friends. That is just imbecilic.

ANIMAL ACTIVIST: Of course animals are my friends. I mean, I know

my dog loves me, he waits for me to come home. And when I walk through the front door, he's obviously happy to see me.

DR. IZZY BIZZY: And why do you think that is? Perhaps it is because you feed it, you pet it, you groom it, you clean up its feces, and essentially you give it everything it could ever want. I mean, correct me if I'm wrong, but you do these things, right?

ANIMAL ACTIVIST: Of course I do, I love my dog. And please do not refer to my beloved friend as an "it," he's just like us, and he has feelings too.

DR. IZZY BIZZY: Look, your dog doesn't "love" you; it likes food, you give it food, and not only do you give it food, but you supply everything else the dog could possibly ever want; of course it is excited when you come home. But the excited response you witness is just simple behavioral conditioning, which you then interpret and personify as similar to the human feeling of "love."

ANIMAL ACTIVIST: No, you're wrong, how can you know that? Can you read my dog's mind?

DR. IZZY BIZZY: Not at all, but you apparently fail to realize that you are also subject to your own asinine point. You obviously know that humans can't read the minds of animals, and yet you simultaneously claim to know what animals "feel" and "want"—which is ridiculous. Animals are just instinctual bundles of reactions; they have no "mind" to read. They show no conscious judgment or decision-making capabilities apart from their instincts and what they've been trained to do.

ANIMAL ACTIVIST: How can you know that? Just because you can't think out of your little "scientific" box, that doesn't mean that my dog can't love me. My dog is excited when I come home because he knows me and he loves me and he's been thinking about me all day.

DR. IZZY BIZZY: Okay . . . that's just crazy talk. Even if it were true that your dog could "think" about you . . . it would only be thinking about the food you are going to give it. And I am willing to wager that if you didn't treat your dog as if it were a god, it wouldn't be so excited to see you when you got home.

STARVING SOMALI: I got excited one time . . . boy, that was a good peanut. . . .

ANIMAL ACTIVIST: You just don't understand because animals don't love people like you. An animal would never care about somebody who isn't an animal lover.

RALPH: I know I love 'em!

ANIMAL ACTIVIST: Good!

RALPH: Nothing hits the spot better than a nice slab of meat. Animals are great!

DR. IZZY BIZZY: Ralph, do you have a dog?

RALPH: Hell yeah, D-Kap Rex kicks ass!

DR. IZZY BIZZY: And do you feed him?

RALPH: Dude . . . we totally feed it beer mixed with his food all the time and like, he gets seriously wasted!

DR. IZZY BIZZY: Ri-i-i-ght . . . And does your dog seem excited to see you when you come home?

RALPH: Well . . . after B-Reed hot-boxed the doghouse when ol' DKR was in there . . . the little bugger just hasn't been the same; he just lays around staring at the wall. But you know, it's pretty sweet.

ANIMAL ACTIVIST: Oh! That's horrible, how can you do that to your dog?

RALPH: What? Dude, Rex loves it, man. A little shmoky shmoke, downing a few brews, and sometimes we let him hump the couch. I mean, c'mon, could you think of a better life?

ANIMAL ACTIVIST: Yes! I could. You've got it all wrong, dogs need whole organic foods, bi-weekly spiritual cleansing, polarity massages, and canine yoga! What you are doing is unnaturally cruel, how can you feed him such unhealthy food?

STARVING SOMALI: Aww, food . . .

DR. IZZY BIZZY: Look, can't you see that you are both just personifying your own personal values onto these animals? Do you really think that dogs want to do keg stands or have their chi focused? Of course not, they want to eat, drink, and hump; that's the way the natural kingdom works.

RALPH: Hell, yeah, dude! The natural kingdom rocks!

ANIMAL ACTIVIST: No, you're wrong! They have a right to live their lives as they see fit, just like you or me.

DR. IZZY BIZZY: All of the "rights" you think that animals "have just like us" are simply the ridiculous personified values you *give* to the animal.

ANIMAL ACTIVIST: What?! No one has the power to "give" rights; they are self-evident truths. They must be fought for and won from oppressors like you. Animals have the *right* to fight for their freedom.

DR. IZZY BIZZY: And you actually think that animals are fighting for these "rights"? I haven't seen too many picketing chickens lately.

ANIMAL ACTIVIST: Well, that's why we have to fight for them, they need our help! Just like any other oppressed slaves.

Dr. Izzy Bizzy: Okay . . . but unlike other real and important movements for human freedom . . . these animal "slaves" will never support or even care about your cause. In all actuality, many of them would probably eat you if they could.

Starving Somali: I'd eat you if I could. . . .

Animal Activist: No, my cause is their cause! Unlike you, I understand that the suffering will end only when we achieve total animal liberation! Then humans and animals will live in balanced spiritual harmony, and we'll truly have peace and oneness and a connection to our mother earth.

Starving Somali: Um, would someone mind swatting these flies off of my eyes?

Ralph: Yeah, I got ya, bro, here you go, (*smack*) no worries.

Animal Activist: Murderer!

Dr. Izzy Bizzy: Wait, wait, wait, I just can't believe that you honestly think that the world would be better off if all animals achieve "total liberation."

Animal Activist: Can't you see that this is the next important fight against slavery?

Dr. Izzy Bizzy: Do you realize the implications of your demands? The billions upon billions of animals in the world can't *all* live together with the billions upon billions of humans in the world. There simply aren't enough resources to feed and sustain all those living species. Something has to give.

Animal Activist: You're wrong, there's more than enough food to feed everyone! Don't you know that we have so much that we have to *pay* farmers to destroy whole storehouses of food!

STARVING SOMALI: Wha, wha, . . . what!?

DR. IZZY BIZZY: Yeah, but a lot of that "food" is produced by animals! Milk and eggs and meat! Look, our whole way of life would change if we just let all these animals roam free! Not only would we lose most of what we eat, we would lose all of the other valuable products that come from animals, like clothing, drugs, cosmetics, fuel. . . .

ANIMAL ACTIVIST: So what? All those barbaric things *should* go!

DR. IZZY BIZZY: Look, the majority of what we consume is somehow related to the so called "exploitation" of animals. Even beer uses chemicals derived from animals in the brewing process.

ANIMAL ACTIVIST: If it causes the exploitation of animals, well, then it needs to go.

RALPH: Now you've just crossed the line!

ANIMAL ACTIVIST: Any form of exploitation of animals is wrong! As a civilized society, we cannot tolerate such unethical practices.

RALPH: Wait, didn't you say you, like, firebomb people's places or something?

ANIMAL ACTIVIST: If we have to use some force to stop the countless deaths of living beings, then so be it! Am I the only one here thinking about what is *right*?! How would you like it if somebody kept you in a cage all of your life and then butchered you for food?

DR. IZZY BIZZY: Your whole argument is based on a false analogy. You try to sway people emotionally with the false idea that animals can experience and "feel" just like humans.

ANIMAL ACTIVIST: Says you!

Dr. Izzy Bizzy: Look, have you ever eaten boiled carrots?

Animal Activist: Yes, but only organic environmentally friendly ones.

Dr. Izzy Bizzy: So how would you feel if somebody chopped you up, boiled you, and then ate you?

Animal Activist: Well, that's not the same.

Dr. Izzy Bizzy: How so?

Animal Activist: Because I'm different from a carrot.

Dr. Izzy Bizzy: Right, and there are important differences between humans and animals. Look, it doesn't make sense to form a moral argument based on comparisons between humans and other species, *precisely because* they are not the same species. For example, the praying mantis eats its partner while mating, but would that make it okay for someone to eat you during sex?

Ralph: Depends on how hot the chick was . . . I mean are we talking about just any average chick, or, like, Britney Spears here? But this crazy chick doesn't even have to worry about it, who would sex her, she stinks like patchouli.

Starving Somali: Well, my standards aren't too high right now. If it meant I got to eat something . . . I'd have sex with her.

Ralph: Word, right on . . . So you trying to play wingman later? 'Cause I've been gunning for this one chick for a while, but the honey totally rolls with this grenade that needs jumping on, a real cow. . . . You know what I'm saying, bro?

Starving Somali: Not at all . . . but I would love some of that honey, chicken, or cow you were talking about. . . . I'd eat anything right now. . . .

save toby! 85

ANIMAL ACTIVIST: Ahem! I don't appreciate your chauvinistic and derogatory comments about women.

RALPH: Huh?

ANIMAL ACTIVIST: Referring to women as "chicks" or "cows" is not right, it's offensive and degrading.

DR. IZZY BIZZY: Hahahaha, this is great. So now you think it's wrong to compare humans to animals?! I thought you just said animals were "just like us" . . . but apparently you also think there is something "offensive" and "degrading" about saying a woman is "just like" a cow.

RALPH: Dude, she's definitely a sister in Phi Moooooo.

ANIMAL ACTIVIST: This is not the same thing, there's a difference. . . .

DR. IZZY BIZZY: Right! There's a fundamental difference between animals and humans. And it's offensive to reduce the importance of a human life to that of a mindless beast.

STARVING SOMALI: Ohhhh . . . fading fast

ANIMAL ACTIVIST: Maybe animals and humans aren't completely the same, but exploiting animals just isn't right!

DR. IZZY BIZZY: No, what's right is whatever is good for humans, as I've already said, there is a— Huh?

RALPH: Whoa! The stick dude totally passed out! I didn't even see him drinking anything.

MODERATOR: Holy crap! He's not drunk, you idiot, he's gone into shock. . . . What happened, nobody gave this kid some food during this whole discussion? Didn't you all get free bag lunches when you came in?

ANIMAL ACTIVIST: Oh, yeah, I threw those away before everyone came in. Those meals had animal flesh in them!

MODERATOR: Quick, grab a sandwich out of the trash and bring it to this kid!

DR. IZZY BIZZY: I got it. . . . Here you go, son. . . .

ANIMAL ACTIVIST: Nooooo, you can't do that! I won't allow it! Flesh eaters!!!

MODERATOR: Wait, what's that you have in your hand? . . . Christ! It's a bomb!

ANIMAL ACTIVIST: I warned you . . . I can't allow your oppression to continue. Long live all life!

DR. IZZY BIZZY: Now this *really* is illogical! . . . How can you claim to support "all life" and then—

BANG

SUPPORT@SAVETOBY.COM . . . and that's where the transcription ends. Good thing I left early to go spend some time with Toby.

FUN FACTS

Actual quote from PETA-payrolled orator Gary Yourofsky (who has spent time in maximum-security prison for animal liberation front crimes): "I have been arrested 13 times for random acts of kindness and compassion. Following in the footsteps of other routine lawbreakers like Dr Martin Luther King Jr., Mohandas Gandhi, Nelson Mandela, and Jesus."

Actual quote from the vice president of PETA, MaryBeth Sweetland: "I'm an insulin-dependent diabetic. Twice a day I take synthetically manufactured insulin that still contains some animal products—and I have no qualms about it. . . . I'm not going to take the chance of killing myself by not taking insulin. I don't see myself as a hypocrite. I need my life to fight for the rights of animals." (from *Glamour*, January 1990)

Worldwatch reports that annual expenditures on pet food in the United States and Europe total $17 billion a year; the estimated cost of immunizing every child, providing clean drinking water for all, and achieving universal literacy is $16.3 billion. The estimate to eliminate hunger and malnutrition worldwide is $19 billion.

Anatomy of an Opportunity

MANY PEOPLE HAVE CONTACTED US ABOUT HOW THEY TOO CAN COME UP WITH A GREAT IDEA FOR MAKING MONEY. The simple answer is, we don't know. The Save Toby! idea was the culmination of years of extortion, the luck of finding Toby under the porch, a case of the High Life, and a moment of pure genius.

Now there are other factors that aided in our success (fingers crossed). Toby is an exceptionally photogenic animal, and obviously the existence of the Internet was crucial in getting the word out. I

mean, imagine trying to execute this scheme ten years ago with a ham radio or a hundred years ago with carrier pigeons.

We have learned some lessons that we can pass on about running a successful Internet scheme. Hopefully, you will find them helpful in executing—sorry, accomplishing—your scheme.

1. Choose your URL wisely

Some of our first choices were less than great. It wasn't until we hit on the simple and catchy SaveToby.com that things really took off. Some of the early URLs that we tried were really quite cumbersome and very difficult to remember. For example:

www.Wewant50korwekillarabbitwefoundyesterday.com
www.Sendussomecashorthebunnygetsit.com
www.Thebenefactionofthelepusamericanus.com
www.geocities.com/~savetoby
www.SaveToby.net

2. Don't be afraid to extend your deadline

Trust me when I say that giving your scheme a countdown is essential. There is no substitute for the sense of urgency that a looming deadline provides, but nothing says "we really want this to work" like an extension. It also gives you more time to make money.

3. Make the stakes high

Death is the ultimate wager, but it isn't the only thing. Try threatening to destroy a priceless artifact, or better yet, find people who think that a camera can steal their soul and threaten to take photos of them.

Just be careful not to break any laws. Destroying things you own is fine, but if you were to say, threaten to burn down the Capitol Building, you wouldn't see a dime. More likely, you'd get thrown in jail and have your lower G.I. tract rearranged by force.

What's important here is that you have to focus on things that can't be fixed or undone. I doubt we would have made much money if we had threatened to *shave* Toby.

4. Get the word out

This point really can't be stressed enough. I mean, if you don't get out there and promote, who is going to do it? If you don't believe in your cause, who will? Look at those e-mail scams where the widow of an ousted African leader is looking for someone to help launder money. She doesn't have other people sending out the e-mails. They come straight from Mrs. Motumbatu herself.

So that's it. Get out there and start marketing. People are sitting out there waiting to give you their money. Are you man enough to take it? Like P. T. Barnum said, "There's a sucker born every minute." Look how many people paid to see *Meet the Fockers*. If you can't get a few bucks off those idiots, you aren't really trying.

Toby-Aid, The Album

FOR MONTHS, WE'VE BEEN TRYING TO ORGANIZE A BENEFIT CONCERT FOR TOBY, and just recently, we were able to finalize the contracts. The show will include many big names. It's really quite exciting. We are already planning the double-disc live album, and I can give you some of the artists and songs that are committed. Two of the artists have even agreed to perform songs written especially for Toby.

Run DMC, who called it quits after the murder of Jam Master Jay have even agreed to reunite for this one special event. Their new song "Save Toby!" is a heartfelt tribute to both Toby and their fallen friend Jam Master Jay. Here is a sample of the touching lyrics:

RUN DMC, SAVE TOBY!

There's a *little* rabbit that *we* all know,
They *call him Toby* and he *needs* some *dough*.
He needs your *help* so he can *be* set *free*,
And be *released* from cap-*tiv*-a-*tee*.

They *say* if you *don't pay* he ain't *gonna* live,
So *reach* in yo' *pockets* and start to *give*.
You can *do* what *you* can to *save Toby*,
And *be* like our *crew*, *Run* D-*M*-C.

So you can *step* right up *to the* plate,
Come with *heavy pockets* and *throw* your *weight*.
We'll *toss it* out *to ya*, so don't *back off*,
Keep your *eye* on the *ball* like *Bil*-et-*nik*-off.

So *gather up* some *ends* and hit up *Am*-azon,
Save a *bunny* from an *early* trip to *the beyond*.
Cause it *ain't right* and it *ain't fair*,
Time *to show* this *hare* how *much you* care.

If there's an *ounce* of *compassion* inside *your* soul,
Make *savin'* this *rabbit* your number-*one* goal.
You can *send a check* or just buy the *book*,
One or *the other*, but don't *let him* cook.

If we don't *save* his *ass* he's *gonna* fry,
It ain't *no joke* Toby's *gonna die*.

If we don't *meet* their *demands* of an *upfront fee*,
Toby's *gonna be* part of a *new* rec-*i*-pe.

So send some *cash* or make a *call* and *use your* clout,
Do what *you can* to get *Toby out*.
Cause if *he's* set *free* and isn't in a *stew*,
You'll know it was all because of *you*.

Elton John is never one to shy away from profiteering on death, so he was an easy sell. Initially, he wanted to do yet another "update" of "Candle in the Wind," but when we told him that Toby wasn't dead yet, he decided an updated version of his classic "Jack Rabbit" was more appropriate. Here are the lyrics.

ELTON JOHN, TOBY RABBIT

Go Toby-rabbit running through the wood
You had a good night and you feel real loose
Heard they got you going round the old goosecreek
Trying to fill their belly full of rabbit meat

Go Toby-rabbit get to the cabbage patch
The guys want to sell a lot of their book
And if they don't you're going to cook
Better go Toby-rabbit better start to run

Go Toby-rabbit running through the wood
You had a good night and you feel real loose
Chef's knife breaking up the peaceful spot
Toby-rabbit sitting in the cooking pot.

OTHER SONGS FROM THE ALBUM:

Jethro Tull, *The Story of the Hare Who Lost His Spectacles*

Big & Rich, *Save a Rabbit (Ride a Cowboy)*

The Moody Blues, *Tortoise and the Hare*

Bright Eyes, *Down in a Rabbit Hole*

Ted Nugent, *F**k Toby, Let's Eat*

Eminem, *Rabbit Run*

Blues Traveler, *Save His Soul*

Tupac, *Save Toby in 2005*

Dusty Springfield, *Save Me Save Me*

Bob Seger, *I Can't Save You Toby*

Cinderella, *Somebody Save Me*

Dr. Dre and Snoop Dogg, *Bitches Ain't S**t*

All profits from the concert and the album will of course go to saving Toby.

An Ode to Toby

My father's name was Lenny—

But this isn't of mice and men—
This is of rabbits,
Or, actually,
One rabbit
My rabbit,
Named Toby.

A rabbit, a friend, a brother I rescued from the cold
Because I love the rabbits like my father did.

So much.

Sooooooo much.

But not as much as money.

(My father was a retard.)

Greedy, yes. But hungry, too!

Starving. And poor.

Have you ever seen *Roger & Me*, Toby?
Have you ever been clubbed with a blunt instrument and
    skinned on camera before?

Of course not; you're my sweet Toby.

A friendly little bunny.

(Atkins friendly, that is.)

My best friend.
Or at least the friend I most want to
Marinate in balsamic dressing and
Spike into a red-hot frying pan.

The hiss and pop of your lean muscle tissue . . .
mmmmm-MMMM!

I can almost taste the friendship!

Toby,
I show you my love with my loving hands

But if and when your time should come
Because I haven't received my money
I'm going to do some horrible things to you.
But they'll be horrible for me, too.
So here's the deal:

Don't think of it as me eating you, my friend . . .

Think of it as me petting you

One last time

With my teeth.

Prayers For Toby

O Lord, creator of the universe, author of its laws, you can bring the dead back to life, and heal those who are sick. We pray for Toby that he may feel your hand upon him, renewing his body and refreshing his soul. Show to him the affection in which you hold all your creatures. *Amen.*

Our Father in heaven, hallowed be your name, your kingdom come, your will be done on earth as it is in heaven.
Give us today our daily bread.

Forgive us our debts, as we also have forgiven our debtors.

And lead us not into temptation, but deliver us from the evil one. And please save Toby.

Amen.

For this reason I kneel before the Father, from whom his whole family in heaven and earth derives its name. I pray that out of his glorious riches he may strengthen you with power though his Spirit in your inner being, so that Christ may dwell in your hearts through faith. And I pray that you, being rooted and established in love, may have power, together with all the saints, to grasp how wide and long and high and deep is the love of Christ, and to know this love that surpasses knowledge—that you may be filled to the measure of all the fullness of God. And that your true believers do then purchase enough books to spare the life of one of your creatures, Toby. *Amen.*

Lord make me an instrument of thy peace!
Where there is hatred, let me sow love;
Where there is injury, pardon;
Where there is doubt, faith;
Where there is despair, hope;
Where there is darkness, light;
Where there is sadness, joy.
Where there is a Save Toby book, buy.
Amen.

Recipe Section

(The Toby Cookbook)

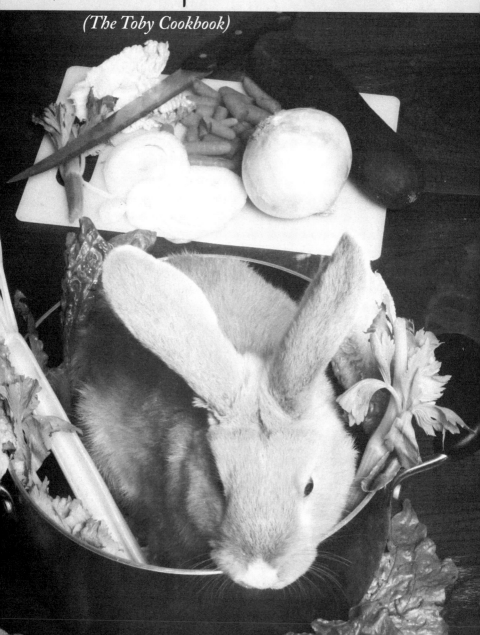

BARBECUE TOBY BURGERS WITH CREAMY COLE SLAW

For burgers
¼ cup Worcestershire sauce
¼ cup ketchup
2 tablespoons soy sauce
2 garlic cloves, minced and
    mashed to a paste with ½ teaspoon salt
1 teaspoon chili powder
¼ teaspoon ground cumin
¼ teaspoon Tabasco
2 pounds ground Toby
1 small onion, minced
½ cup fresh bread crumbs

For cole slaw
⅓ cup mayonnaise
2 tablespoons cider vinegar
1 tablespoon sugar
1 teaspoon Dijon mustard
3 cups finely shredded cabbage
1 large carrot, shredded coarse
1 small red onion, sliced thin

6 6-inch pitas, split open to form pockets

Make burgers: In a small bowl stir together Worcestershire sauce, ketchup, soy sauce, garlic paste, chili powder, cumin, Tabasco, and salt and pepper to taste until sauce is smooth. In a large bowl stir together Toby, onion, bread crumbs, and ¼ cup sauce until combined well and form into six ¾-inch-thick patties. Toby Burgers may be prepared up to this point 1 day ahead and chilled, covered. Divide remaining sauce in half and put in separate bowls, half for brushing Toby on the grill and half for drizzling on cooked burgers. Chill sauce, covered.

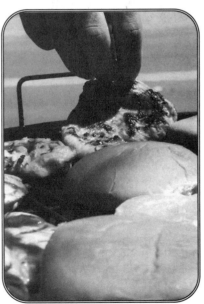

Make cole slaw: In a large bowl whisk together mayonnaise, vinegar, sugar, and mustard. Add remaining cole slaw ingredients and salt and pepper to taste, and toss to combine well. Cole slaw may be made 4 hours ahead and chilled, covered.

Prepare grill. Grill Toby Burgers on an oiled rack set 5 to 6 inches over glowing coals, brushing frequently with barbecue sauce, 6 minutes on each side, or until cooked through. Drizzle Toby Burgers with remaining barbecue sauce and serve with cole slaw in pita pockets.

Makes 6 servings.

BARBECUED TOBY PIZZA

This terrific dish also works well as an appetizer if it's cut into bite-size pieces.

3 tablespoons olive oil
1 Toby, de-boned and
   cut into small pieces
1 cup diced onion
1 large zucchini, halved lengthwise, seeded, cut into ½-inch cubes
½ large yellow crookneck squash,
   halved lengthwise, seeded, cut into ½-inch cubes
2 cups (packed) shredded mozzarella cheese (about 8 ounces)
⅓ cup plus 3 tablespoons chopped fresh cilantro

1 10-ounce pre-made fully baked thin pizza crust (such as Boboli)
6 tablespoons bottled barbecue sauce

Preheat oven to 450°F. Heat 2 tablespoons oil in heavy medium skillet over medium-high heat. Season Toby with salt and pepper. Sauté Toby until cooked through, about 5 minutes per side. Transfer Toby to cutting board. Cut Toby into ½-inch cubes; place Toby in large bowl.

Add remaining 1 tablespoon oil and onion to same skillet; sauté over medium-high heat 2 minutes. Add zucchini and yellow squash; sauté until tender but still crisp, about 4 minutes. Transfer vegetable mixture to bowl with Toby and cool. Mix in cheese and ⅓ cup cilantro. Season topping to taste with salt and pepper.

Place pizza crust on large baking sheet. Spread 4 tablespoons barbecue sauce over crust. Top with Toby mixture. Drizzle with remaining 2 tablespoons sauce. Bake pizza until heated through and cheese melts, about 15 minutes. Sprinkle with remaining 3 tablespoons cilantro and serve.

Makes 4 main-course servings.

BRAISED TOBY WITH EGG NOODLES

More supermarkets are carrying fresh rabbit, but since we have our own fresh rabbit we don't have to worry about trying to find one. Braising will help to keep Toby moist and tender.

1 Toby, cut into 8 serving pieces
1 teaspoon salt
½ teaspoon black pepper
¼ cup extra-virgin olive oil
2 medium onions, halved lengthwise,
   then cut lengthwise into ¼-inch slices
2 garlic cloves, chopped fine
2 (4 x 1-inch) strips fresh orange zest
1 (3- to 4-inch) cinnamon stick

2 Turkish bay leaves (or 1 California)
½ cup dry red wine
2 cups canned crushed tomatoes
   (from a 28-ounce can)
½ cup water
8 ounces dried egg tagliatelle
   or egg fettuccine
1 tablespoon chopped
   fresh flat-leaf parsley

Special equipment: A deep 12-inch ovenproof skillet (preferably with a lid) or a 5-quart wide heavy pot.

Preheat oven to 350°F.

Pat Toby pieces dry and sprinkle with ½ teaspoon salt and ¼ teaspoon pepper. Heat 2 tablespoons oil in skillet over medium-high heat until hot but not smoking, then brown Toby in 2 batches, turning over once, about 6 minutes per batch. Transfer as browned to a plate.

Reduce heat to medium and cook onions, garlic, zest, cinnamon stick, and bay leaves in remaining 2 tablespoons oil, stirring frequently, until onions are beginning to brown, 4 to 5 minutes. Add wine and deglaze skillet by boiling, stirring and scraping up any brown bits, until wine is reduced by about half, about 2 minutes. Stir in tomatoes, water, remaining ½ teaspoon salt, and remaining ¼ teaspoon pepper. Nestle Toby pieces in sauce and bring to a simmer.

Cover skillet tightly with lid or heavy-duty foil, then braise in middle of oven 30 minutes. Turn Toby over and continue to braise, covered, until he is tender, 25 to 30 minutes more.

While Toby is braising, cook pasta in a large pot of boiling salted water until al dente. Drain pasta well in a colander and transfer to a large platter. Discard zest, cinnamon stick, and bay leaf from sauce. Arrange Toby over pasta, then spoon sauce over top and sprinkle with parsley.

Cooks' note: Toby can be braised 1 day ahead and cooled, uncovered, then chilled, covered. Reheat on top of stove until hot.

Makes 4 servings.

CURRIED TOBY

Serve Toby with steamed white rice and Indian beer, and make a stop at an Indian restaurant to get some samosas—savory filled pastries—to pass as appetizers, and the flatbread called naan to sop up the curry sauce. For dessert, how about assorted teas and a carrot cake?

3 tablespoons vegetable oil
3 cups chopped onions
¼ cup minced peeled fresh ginger
3 garlic cloves, minced
3 tablespoons curry powder
1 teaspoon ground cumin
¼ teaspoon ground cinnamon
2 tablespoons all-purpose flour
1 cup plain yogurt
3 tablespoons tomato paste
3 cups canned low-salt chicken broth
1 cup unsweetened applesauce

1 Toby de-boned and cut up crossways
    into 1-inch slices
1 10-ounce package frozen peas
½ cup sour cream
½ cup canned unsweetened coconut milk*
Fresh cilantro sprigs
Steamed white rice
Major Grey mango chutney
Sliced peeled bananas
Chopped pitted peeled mangoes
Shredded unsweetened coconut
Chopped toasted peanuts

Heat oil in heavy large pot over medium heat. Add onions and sauté until golden, about 15 minutes. Add ginger and garlic; sauté 1 minute. Add curry powder, cumin, and cinnamon; sauté until fragrant, about 1 minute. Add flour, then yogurt and tomato paste, whisking until sauce is smooth, about 1 minute. Add broth and applesauce. Bring to boil. Reduce heat; simmer until sauce thickens slightly, stirring occasionally, about 30 minutes. (Can be made 1 day ahead. Cool slightly. Cover and chill. Bring to simmer before continuing.)

Add Toby and peas to sauce. Simmer until Toby is almost cooked through, about 3 minutes. Add sour cream and coconut milk. Reduce heat to medium low. Stir until Toby is cooked through and sauce thickens enough to coat spoon, about 3 minutes (do not boil). Season with salt and pepper. Transfer to bowl. Garnish with cilantro sprigs.

Place rice, chutney, bananas, mangoes, coconut, and peanuts in separate bowls. Serve alongside curry.

Makes 8–10 servings.

SPICY TOBY CHILI

2 tablespoons olive oil
1 Toby, cleaned and de-boned
1 green pepper, diced
1 onion, diced
2 cloves garlic
2 15-ounce cans diced tomatoes

1 can black beans
1 can red kidney beans
2 tablespoons dark brown sugar
1 tablespoon chili powder
1 tablespoon cumin
1 tsp chipotle hot sauce

*Available at Indian, Southeast Asian and Latin American markets and at many supermarkets.

106 SAVE tOBY!

Heat olive oil in large skillet, add Toby and brown. Add green pepper, onion, and garlic and cook until slightly brown. Add remaining ingredients and reduce heat to simmer, cover and cook for 1 hour or until Toby is tender.

Serve with sweet corn bread.

Wine pairing: Rabbit Ridge Le Lapin, Sonoma County Reserve

TOBY TERRINE WITH GREEN OLIVES AND PISTACHIOS

For Toby and broth
1 Toby, cut into 8 pieces
4 shallots, sliced thin
2 carrots, sliced thin
3 fresh parsley sprigs
2 fresh thyme sprigs
1 leek (green part only), rinsed
1 head garlic, left unpeeled and halved
   horizontally
½ teaspoon black peppercorns, cracked
½ teaspoon salt
6¼ cups cold water
2 large egg whites plus shells, crushed
4 teaspoons unflavored gelatin (from
   two ¼-ounce envelopes)
1 tablespoon Madeira

For assembling terrines
½ teaspoon fennel seeds, toasted*
½ cup picholine or other brine-cured green
   olives (3 ounces), pitted and coarsely
   chopped
⅓ cup salted shelled pistachios, coarsely
   chopped
3 tablespoons thinly sliced fresh chives
1 teaspoon chopped fresh thyme
½ teaspoon salt
¾ teaspoon black pepper

Accompaniment: 18 very thin slices firm white sandwich bread, each slice buttered and cut into 2 pieces the shape of terrine slices, then toasted.**
Special equipment: 2 (12 x 2-inch) tapered narrow rectangular terrines; kitchen string; 2 (11½ x 1½-inch) strips of corrugated cardboard wrapped well with foil; 2 (10- to 11-inch) rolling pins or high-shouldered wine bottles.

* Toast spices in a dry heavy skillet over moderate heat, stirring, until fragrant and a shade or two darker.
** To toast, arrange bread slices on a baking sheet and spread with 2 tablespoons butter. Toast in middle of oven until golden, about 10 minutes.

Cook Toby in broth: Remove fat, kidneys, and liver from Toby. Put Toby, shallots, carrots, parsley, thyme, leek, garlic, peppercorns, ¼ teaspoon salt, and 6 cups water in a 4-quart heavy pot and bring to a boil, skimming froth. Reduce heat and gently simmer Toby, partially covered, until tender, 1 hour.

Clarify broth: Cool Toby in broth, uncovered, 30 minutes, then remove, reserving Toby pieces and broth separately. Pour broth through a fine sieve into a bowl, discarding solids. Whisk egg whites in another bowl until foamy and add egg shells. Whisk in warm broth in a stream and return mixture to cleaned pot.

Heat over moderate heat, stirring and scraping bottom constantly with a wooden spoon to prevent egg white from sticking, until stock comes to a simmer (about 10 minutes). Reduce heat and gently simmer broth, without stirring, until all impurities rise to surface and form a crust, and broth underneath is clear, about 10 minutes.

While broth is simmering, coarsely shred Toby's meat, being careful to remove all small bones.

Pour broth through a sieve lined with a double thickness of dampened paper towels into a bowl, and let all broth drain through. Discard solids. (If liquid doesn't drain completely, tap edge of sieve repeatedly with a metal spoon to help drain.) Broth should be completely clear; if not, repeat procedure with clean dampened paper towels.

If clarified broth measures more than 2½ cups, boil to reduce. If it measures less, add water. Bring broth just to a simmer. Sprinkle gelatin over remaining ¼ cup cold water and soften 1 minute, then whisk into hot broth until dissolved. Stir in Madeira and remaining ¼ teaspoon salt, or to taste.

Assemble terrines: Lightly oil terrines and line with a sheet of plastic wrap large enough to drape over edges. Place terrines on a tray. Cut 4 18-inch pieces of kitchen string and place 2 crosswise under each terrine about 2 inches from each end (they will be used to secure rolling pins or bottles to terrines).

Grind fennel seeds with a mortar and pestle or in an electric coffee/spice grinder and toss with Toby, olives, pistachios, chives, thyme, salt, and pepper in a large bowl. Divide mixture between terrines, then stir broth well and pour slowly into terrines, filling to ¼ inch from top. Reserve any remaining broth, covered and chilled. Place a foil-wrapped cardboard strip on top of each terrine, then rest a rolling pin or bottle on top of cardboard and tie to terrine, creating just enough pressure to press cardboard about ½ inch into terrine (some broth will spill over onto tray).

Chill terrines on tray 3 hours, then remove string, weights, and cardboard. Heat any reserved jelled broth (including spillover on tray) just until it becomes liquid and add to terrines. Cover with overhanging plastic wrap and chill at least 6 hours more.

To unmold terrines, unwrap plastic wrap and invert molds onto a long narrow platter, pulling slightly on plastic to release terrines from molds, then removing it. Gently cut terrines with a serrated knife into ⅓-inch-thick slices and serve on pieces of toast.

Cook's notes: **1.** Terrines may be chilled up to 3 days.
2. If you'd like to serve the terrines already cut and on pieces of toast, you can conveniently make them in a baking pan rather than terrine molds. You'll need two 13 x 9-inch pans: Line one pan as for terrines (you will need two well-overlapping lengths of

plastic wrap) and spread all of Toby mixture and broth evenly in pan. Cover with more plastic wrap and gently press second 13 x 9-inch pan on top. Distribute 3 pounds of weight (such as three 1-pound cans) in pan and chill terrine until completely firm, at least 4 hours. Remove weights, top pan, and top layer of plastic wrap and invert onto a cutting board. Remove remaining plastic wrap and cut terrine into 1¼-inch squares with a long sharp knife.

Makes about 40 hors d'oeuvres.

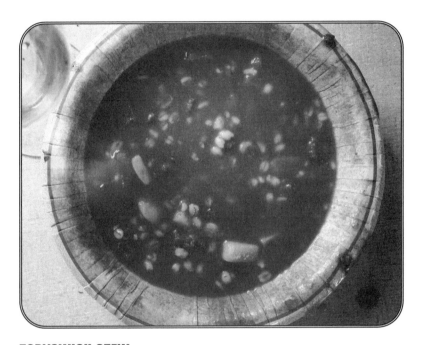

TOBYSWICK STEW

1 Toby, cleaned and quartered
1 large yellow onion, chopped
3 cloves garlic, minced
2 cups frozen lima beans
2 cups frozen yellow corn
1 16-ounce can chopped tomatoes

2 tablespoons sugar
1 tablespoon salt
1 teaspoon pepper
2 bay leaves
4 tablespoons oil

Heat oil in a large pot, then add onions and garlic and cook until translucent.

Add Toby and enough water to just cover him. Bring to a boil, add salt, pepper and bay leaves. Reduce heat and cook till Toby falls off his bones. Strain Toby through colander and reserve liquid.

Separate Toby from his bones and discard bones. Return Toby to pot with reserved liquid. Add lima beans, corn, and tomatoes and bring to a slow boil.

Add sugar and cook at low heat for 1 hour. Serve with sweet corn muffins.

Makes 4 servings.

Selected Bibliography

Ducasse, Alain (Feb. 6, 2002). "Les Lapins sont délicieux!" *Mangez, mangez, mangez!* p.57.

Fossey, Dian (1985). *Bunnies in the Mist,* p.137.

Gester, Paul (Aug. 7, 2003). "From Snails to Cottontails: The French Will Eat Anything." *Journal of Outlaw Sauces,* p.77.

Goldberg, Gary David (March 19, 1987). "My Name Is Alex" episode of *Family Ties,* scene 12: "Alex strangles a bunny with his bare hands and eats it raw" (scene deleted from American release).

Grafton, Sue (1995). *R is for Rabbit Hostage.*

Levi-Strauss, Claude (1964). *Le Lapin cru et le lapin cuit,* p.839.

Moses (13th century BC). *Leviticus, 11:6*

Orton, Michelle (Sept. 9, 2004). "I just saw this website about this bunny—is this a joke?" letsblogaboutbunnies.blogspot.com.

Singer, Peter (Jan. 10, 2005). "Why Don't Bunnies Have the Same Rights As People?" *Journal of Dumb Waah Waah Whining,* p.17.

Acknowledgments

We would like to give special thanks to:

•Al Gore, for inventing the Internet, without which none of this would be possible. Thanks, Al.

•Johannes Gutenberg, because Johannes is pretty much the most bad-ass name ever, you could seriously karate chop through a refrigerator with a name like that, and when you toss a Gutenberg in there, it's just like, man, watch out for that guy, he's going places.

•Dr. Izzy Bizzy, the Asian crime fighter, maintenance man, and philosopher extraordinaire, for his countless hours of toil and effort over this book.

•A guy from Harvard, because he knows a lot more about stuff and things than we know about them and he can also write real good.

•Matthew Heitz, whose countless hours of nay-saying led us to create the greatest book ever known to man. Unfortunately, that one got erased and we were left with this.

•2-1-7, for not caving in or burning down.

•Lucky Seven, for squeezing out our creative juices with the sweet nectar that is a 40-ounce malt liquor such as Steel Reserve.

•The Phat Phree writers, although they weren't free: Mike Martone, Dave Amiott, Bill Hall, Jimmy Colo, Aemilia Scott, Chris Browne, Matthew Meadowbrook, D.V.D., Matthew L. McCoy, and Pasqual Orenthal Timbershoot, Esq.

•Jeremie Ruby-Strauss, or Jer Jer Binks as we have dubbed him, for his help in publishing this book.

save toby!

•Visions, the greatest band ever, and Ren, the greatest keyboardist on the planet!

•Toby, for being the world's greatest bunny, even though he smells like crap and pees on everything and chews through all of our cords, completely ruining our camera. All that and he doesn't even know his own name, but can ya blame him? Yes, actually, we can and we do.

•Kenny G, for his inspirational music.

•Rock-Paper-Scissors, for providing an answer to every conflict or crucial decision regarding this book.